Stockton Memories

Stockton Memories

A Pictorial History of Stockton, California

by R. Coke Wood
and
Leonard Covello

Fresno  1977

STOCKTON MEMORIES
Copyright © 1977 by Valley Publishers

All rights reserved. No part of this book may be reproduced or utilized in any form or by any means without permission in writing, except in the case of brief quotations embodied in critical articles or reviews.

Library of Congress Catalog Card Number 77-82897
ISBN 0-913548-44-8

Published by Valley Publishers
Fresno, California
Printed in the United States of America

Publisher's Preface

When a community is fortunate enough to have a writer-historian of the stature of R. Coke Wood, "Mr. California," and a photographer-historian as dedicated and talented as Leonard Covello, that community is assured of having its history carefully and lovingly recorded.

This book is evidence of the abilities of these two men, whose lives have been closely involved with the city of Stockton and the state of California for many years.

Leonard Covello came with his parents as a small boy from Italy and started his education in 1916 at Fair Oaks School in Stockton. His career was in music; he played in small dance combos and later in night clubs throughout California, but Stockton was always his home.

In 1934 he married Ardath Shackelford, from a pioneer Stockton family. Her grandfather, William McMurry, came across the plains in a covered wagon in 1852.

Leonard's second career, in photography, began in 1941. He learned by trial and error, with the aid of some training in a correspondence school and later a short period at Brooks Institute of Photography in Santa Barbara. His experience and his collection of photographs both increased during the years he spent as a free lance photographer and as a part-time reporter and photographer for the San Francisco *Examiner* in the Stockton area. As his skill developed he became interested in copying and restoring historical pictures taken by several of Stockton's early fine photographers—McCullen, Rulofson, Stuart, Batchelder, Wells, Spooner, Monaco, Logan, and Covert Martin. It was a challenge to make copies from old daguerreotypes, tin types, and glass negatives, a process which requires care and skill.

Leonard's fine collection is based on the best he could recover from earlier photographers and from the hundreds of negatives he has taken in his thirty-six years as a photographer. He has been the official photographer for the San Joaquin County Fair for thirty-one years, and his pictures have appeared in several national publications including *Life* magazine.

In 1969 Dr. R. Coke Wood was honored by the Legislature of the State of California by being proclaimed "Mr. California." He is the embodiment of the spirit of the many people in this state who love it enough to want to know all that has happened here, when, how, and why. Dr. Wood has been teaching California and Western History in Stockton since 1951, most recently as a professor of history at San Joaquin Delta College and the University of the Pacific. He conducted the California Mission Tours for history students for fourteen years, and was one of the founders of the Conference of California Historical Societies. He has been a guiding spirit of that organization for nearly twenty-five years.

As a boy Coke lived in Bishop in Owen's Valley. He graduated from the College of the Pacific in 1932 and in 1950 received his PhD. from the University of Southern California. Due to illness he spent several years in sanatoriums; he finally recovered at the Bret Harte Sanatorium in Murphys in the Mother Lode. His wife is the former Ethelyn Edson, a descendant of pioneer families that settled in Fortuna, Humboldt County. Her grandfather, Absalom Shultz, crossed the plains in 1857. She went to Murphys to teach at the Sanatorium in 1939.

During their twelve years in Murphys the Woods became interested in the history of the little mining town and restored the old P. L. Traver Building there. For twenty-seven years they have operated the Old Timers' Museum. In 1950 they returned to Stockton, but continued to have a great interest in Murphys. To promote this interest Coke has published over twenty books on the history of California. He assisted Covert Martin in organizing his photographs and writing the manuscript for *Stockton Album Through the Years*, published in 1959, another experience which helped qualify him to author this book. He was a consultant in the recent publication of a history of the University of the Pacific during the years of Robert Burns' presidency, *Pioneer or Perish* by Kara Pratt Brewer.

Stockton Memories is a reflection of the affection for their city that is felt by all true Stocktonians, expressed in these pages by two fine representatives, Leonard Covello and Dr. R. Coke Wood.

Introduction

Because the reader should understand the objectives and hopes of the authors in order to fully appreciate a book, we would like to make clear what we have attempted to do in *Stockton Memories*. We were asked by Charles Clough of Valley Publishers to produce a book based on Leonard Covello's extensive collection of historical pictures of Stockton. We were not asked to write a history of Stockton and illustrate it with pictures. There is a great difference in the two objectives.

Our plan then was to select from about a thousand pictures from Leonard's collection of over 25,000 photographs that would tell an interesting story of Stockton's past—a difficult task. To aid us we decided on several categories, each dealing with one of the most significant aspects of Stockton's 127-year history. We agreed that we would not duplicate the same period covered by Covert Martin in *Stockton Album Through the Years*. Since Dr. Wood collaborated with Mr. Martin, there may be some repetition, but our emphasis has been on the more recent history of Stockton, as we wanted to include scenes and events you may remember.

The authors have been friends for many years and both have been involved in preserving California and Stockton history through pictures, writing, teaching, lecturing, and slide shows. We're happy to bring together these experiences in the creation of *Stockton Memories*.

No man is an island and we have had excellent assistance. We must thank Ardath Covello for her courageous and determined effort in recopying and correcting the longhand versions of the manuscript and captions.

We are especially grateful to Raymond W. Hillman, Curator of History at the Pioneer Museum and Haggin Galleries, for his assistance in reading and correcting the manuscript. Through his work at the museum and as an instructor in California History at Delta College, he has become especially well informed about the history of Stockton. Ancestral ties in the community have also contributed to his deep interest in the subject. His critical examination of our writing gives us a feeling of assurance that we have made no major errors.

We hope you enjoy our combined efforts. We know you will call us if you find errors, but let us know also if you like our *Stockton Memories*.

August 1977

Leonard Covello
and
Coke Wood

Table of Contents

1	Development	1
2	Waterways	15
3	Transportation	25
4	Business and Commerce	39
5	Buildings	53
6	Government, Politicians, and Patriotism	59
7	Law Enforcement	71
8	Fire Department	79
9	Agriculture	87
10	Education	99
11	Communications	115
12	Hospitals	125
13	Religion	137
14	Entertainment	145
15	Et Cetera	157
	Index	171

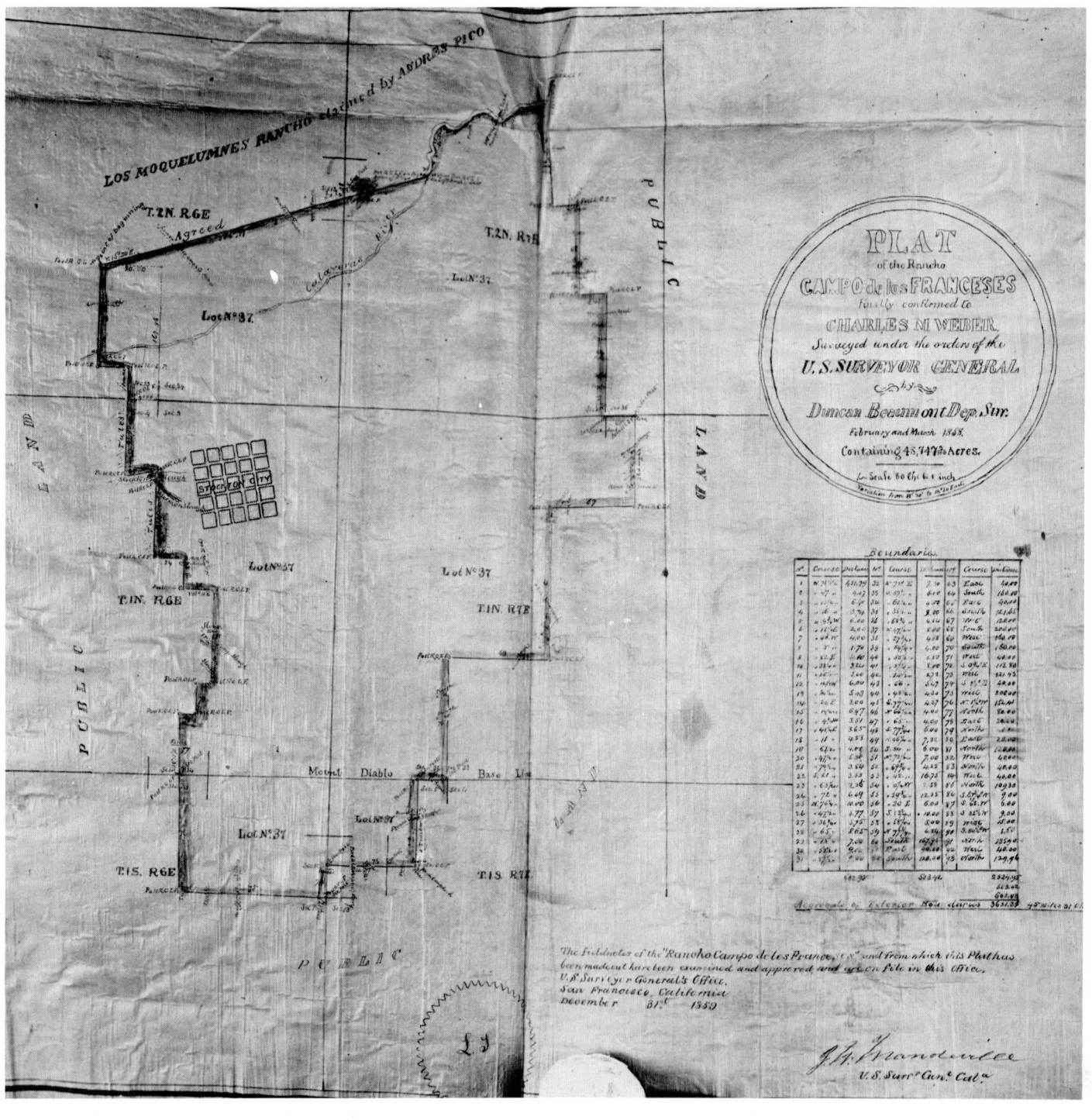

1 Development

Stockton and how it grew from the head of the channel

What a dramatic story could be told, in picture and word, of Stockton's growth, from Captain Weber's first little store at the corner of Center and Levee Streets in 1847 to the present city of 120,000 with its large suburban shopping centers. To tell that story in full, this entire book would have to be devoted to it, and even more pages would be needed. Perhaps, however, by highlighting some of the more important developments, we can adequately tell the story of Stockton's growth.

The head of the channel, where five "sloughs" come together, has traditionally been the heart of the city. This was the head of navigation at El Dorado Street and Weber Avenue. The river boats coming up the San Joaquin River would turn east from the main river channel and bring supplies another two miles to the juncture of these sloughs.

Captain Weber not only located his first store in this area but built an elaborate home here in 1850. This occupied land between McLeod's Lake and the Stockton Channel became known as Weber Point. It was here that the Stockton House, the first hotel, was built. Also located here was the Corinthian Building, location of some of the earliest government offices.

Just a short distance away was land Captain Weber gave for the Plaza, the heart of any Spanish or Mexican town. Stockton's Plaza is Hunter Square. He also gave a square block between Main Street and Weber Avenue on the Plaza for the county courthouse which was constructed in 1853. This became the first "downtown" of Stockton, as businesses grew up around the head of the channel, and gained a greater significance as Stockton became the supply base for the Southern Mines.

In 1869 the City Council refused the demand of the Central Pacific Railroad for adequate land to construct railroad yards and a depot at the head of the channel, calling this demand "exorbitant blackmail." The railroad "by-passed" the city to establish a railroad junction at Lathrop, a few miles to the southeast. Leland Stanford predicted that this by-pass would cause "grass to grow in the streets of Stockton," but Lathrop never prospered and the extensive river traffic bringing supplies from San Francisco maintained the importance of the young city of Stockton.

The Stockton and Copperopolis Railroad built a depot on the south bank of the Stockton Channel in 1871. Flour mills, carriage and wagon factories, iron foundries and shipyards clustered around the channel and its tributaries for many years.

Stockton became not only the supply base for the gold mines but also for a rich agricultural area, especially with the reclamation of delta lands. The large ranches needed farm machinery and farm workers. The "downtown" became larger and the businesses moved further away. The first "downtown" then became known as "Skid Row." As the years rolled by and the decrepit buildings were not replaced or modernized, this area became the center for transients, laborers, drunkards and bums. In the late 1950s and 1960s federal funds became available and cities, including Stockton, began to form redevelopment districts and tear down old substandard and decaying buildings.

Now, in the 1970s, much of this old area has become a new downtown of modern buildings—a new County Courthouse and Administration Building, police facility, Filipino Center, banks, etc. In the plaza is a beautiful fountain that adds charm to the formerly drab area.

Because of the increased use of automobiles the downtown became congested with traffic and new business centers developed in the suburbs of Stockton. One of the first of these was Tuxedo Park on Pacific Avenue. This area had been Lower Sacramento Road until the College of the Pacific moved to Stockton and started building its campus north of the city in 1925. The Tuxedo Park area was influenced by the coming of the Pacific campus but it was more than a business development and many fine homes were built there. Eventually Joe Plecarpo, one of the business leaders and developers, dubbed the business section along Pacific Avenue as the "Miracle Mile."

Started in the 1950s, Lincoln Village was one of the first large suburban real estate and shopping areas to be developed to the north of Stockton along Pacific Avenue.

As downtown parking became more difficult, large department stores began to realize the value of having

This view, c. 1850s, is looking westerly along Channel Street. In the center is the old Weber fire station. The vacant lot used to be the location of the Corinthian Building. McLeod Lake is at the right. At the far left is all that remained of the New York Hotel, one of Stockton's first. Part of the Holiday Inn now occupies its site.

space for large parking lots out in the suburbs. The use of public transportation was abandoned in favor of automobiles, often two or three in one family. The main department stores—Sears, Montgomery Ward, Weinstock's, J. C. Penney, Breuner's, Macy's, etc.—moved northward, and Weberstown and Lincoln Village became more important than the downtown business area. Unfortunately for Stockton's tax rate, these areas have not been annexed into the city limits though they are served in many ways by the city of Stockton.

But the downtown section of Stockton has not given up. New parking lots have been built to serve both new and older buildings in the area, and streets and parking lots are being beautified with shrubs and flowers to invite shoppers to come to "Beautiful Downtown Stockton."

Here is a view of Main Street, looking east from California Street before the street was paved, c. 1890. Austin Brothers Hardware at American and Main Streets later became the location of the J. C. Penney Store. Notice the wooden sidewalks.

Water wagons were employed to keep down dust in the summertime—an essential service before Stockton's streets were paved. Picture c. 1900.

Main Street looking east from Hunter, in the 1890s, above, and in the 1920s, right. Thirty years of growth are apparent—the cobblestone streets have been paved; the horse and buggy have been replaced by the automobile; one of the tallest structures, the spire, has been dwarfed by buildings of greater height; the palm tree to the far left has grown tall.

The cobblestones seen in the earlier view came from Folsom.

Several of the buildings in the later picture are still standing today.

Just before the turn of the century "Lots for Sale" ads appeared in the Stockton newspapers. In those days North Stockton was the area between Harding Way and Oak Park.

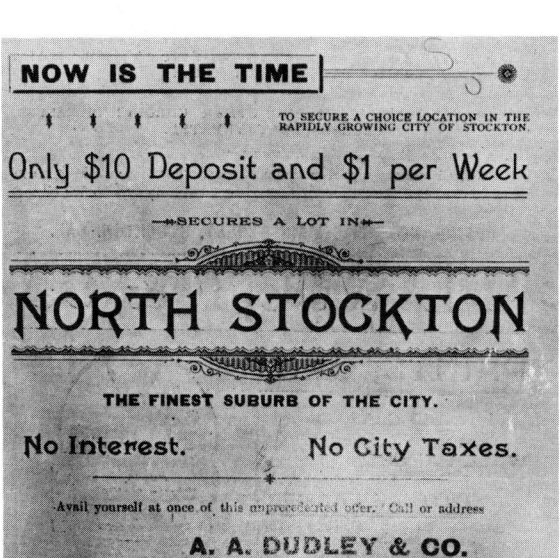

Stockton in 1900, looking north from Main Street on San Joaquin Street. In the far background is the Central Methodist Church. In front of the church is the old county jail and on the right is the lofty Yosemite Building. Near the top of the Yosemite Building can be seen the sign of J. Pitcher Spooner, famous Stockton photographer. This building was torn down in 1972 to make room for an off-street parking lot. Notice the dress styles and the carbon arc electric street lamp.

El Dorado Street and Weber Avenue, about 1915. Stockton was really getting modern, with the Model T Fords, electric streetcars and uniformed policemen. The tallest building on the right is the old Masonic Temple. Radio station KJOY is now located in the old Hotel Stockton building shown at the far right.

In the 1920s the heart of the city was California and Main Streets. It was a busy area at five o'clock in the afternoon with many cars and two sets of streetcar tracks. Notice police officer Benjamin Cassidy directing traffic.

Downtown Stockton in 1923 looking north down California Street from Main. The old Owl Drug Store is remembered by many.

Tuxedo Park about 1919, looking west. The developers boasted thirty-four homes. Pacific Avenue is in foreground; at far left is Smith Canal and part of Yosemite Lake; in center background is Country Club Boulevard running through farm lands to the Stockton Golf and Country Club.

Pacific Avenue looking north, 1923. The Piggly Wiggly Store is to the right. The photographer was V. Covert Martin. Not only did he photograph the scene, but also his camera case alongside his car.

The entrance to Tuxedo Park from Pacific Avenue in 1934. The arch bears the name of the Ford distributors, Althouse Eagal Company. The Milky Way malt shop was a favorite hangout for the college kids. It was in this store that the great hit song "Tuxedo Junction" was written by Al Harkins in the 1940s. (Below)

Ralph Yardley's drawing of the intersection of North Street (Harding Way), Lower Sacramento Road (Pacific Avenue), and Madison Street. Yardley was a Stockton Record artist for many years.

"The Miracle Mile." An air view above Pacific Avenue looking north from Harding Way to Alpine Avenue. The avenue became noted during the 1940s as Stockton's first northern shopping area. Compare the intersection of Harding Way and Pacific Avenue with Ralph Yardley's drawing of earlier days.

Looking north on El Dorado Street from Lafayette in the 1950s, just before redevelopment, this scene is a part of what was known as the old "Skid Row."

Part of the nine-block West End Redevelopment as it was started in about 1966. This partly razed section shows the method of knocking down the old buildings and reducing them to rubble so they could be hauled away easily.

Washington Park, across from old St. Mary's Church. In 1887 it was the location of the San Joaquin Agricultural Society Pavilion, which occupied the entire block. The Pavilion was destroyed by fire sixteen years later. Washington Park was then developed and lasted from 1903 to 1977. Today it is part of the crosstown freeway that heads toward Highway 99.

In these three photographs of Hunter Square Plaza, from the 1880s, 1950s, and 1960s, the only obvious similarities are between the two later ones, but the same building appears in all three—the Mansion House to the far right. It was given a drastic face lift at some time before the '50s.

The Plaza has been the heart of the city since Captain Weber donated the site in the early 1850s.

Facing page: The Civic Center in 1946 when McLeod Lake still led up to El Dorado Street. At left is the Civic Center Auditorium and to the right is City Hall, both built in the mid-1920s. The area was later filled in to Center Street and has become a beautiful park with a fountain.

Interstate 5 is running along the background of this 1977 view. Stockton is one of few cities not by-passed by this freeway. Part of the crosstown freeway headed for Highway 99 can be seen at the left. The construction stopped at Stanislaus Street in 1975.

In 1950 Lincoln Village, upper right, boasted two streets, fewer than thirty homes, and no shopping center. Pacific Avenue is in the foreground. Benjamin Holt Drive runs through the center. Above is an extended view of the same area some twenty-five years later. Interstate 5 divides Lincoln Village and Lincoln Village West.

North Stockton in 1977. This aerial view shows the University of the Pacific campus, Pacific Avenue, and the Calaveras River. In the left foreground is Burns Tower on the University of Pacific campus. In the center is Weberstown shopping center. To the center left is the new campus of San Joaquin Delta College.

An aerial view of Louis Park. The park has a boat launching ramp and features Pixie Woods, a children's fantasy land. The San Joaquin River stretches into the distance.

In 1965 the intersections of Main and San Joaquin Streets and Main and Sutter Streets were painted red, white and blue, to help beautify downtown Stockton. This effort was not completely successful, and later this portion of the city was decorated with scenes of Stockton painted on the backs and sides of some of the buildings. A photograph of San Joaquin and Main as it appeared in 1908 may be seen on page 47.

2 Waterways

Waterways have been of utmost importance in Stockton's history. Sometimes the Delta around Stockton has been called the "Holland of America" because of the estimated eleven hundred miles of waterways. Much of the land in the San Joaquin River delta has been reclaimed by the building of levees to restrict the water channels. These sloughs and river channels are a popular area for water sports and are also used by farmers for irrigating their crops.

Of course the first use of these sloughs and river channels was for navigation, and Stockton has made the most of the opportunity by building California's largest inland port. Leaders of the city began their pre-planning and dreaming of the deep water project as early as 1871 when the Stockton Ship Canal Company was organized and employed R. L. Alexander to make a survey for a deep water channel some fifteen miles long and costing about $3,000,000. The map that was drawn was very convincing but raising such funds locally was too much for the promoters to undertake. However, by 1917 interest was renewed and plans began for a joint endeavor by the federal government and the State of California. Local support was ensured when the people of Stockton enthusiastically endorsed $1,307,000 in Deep Water Bonds in April 1925 by a vote ratio of thirteen to one. These funds would be used largely for acquiring rights of way for the canal and land for the port facilities. The right of way was to be 750 feet wide but the channel would be thirty-two feet deep with a bottom width of one hundred feet. This canal would cut straight across the islands and curves of the river to facilitate navigation for the large ocean-going freighters expected to use the port. A bill passed by Congress supporting the project was signed by President Calvin Coolidge on June 21, 1927.

Construction on the Deep Water Project began with the first shovelfuls of dirt being turned by dragline rigs on West Washington Street in 1928. The dredging was pushed through, bringing deep water to Stockton on

A mighty influence on agriculture, recreation and transportation—from steamboats and sail boats to ocean going vessels

15

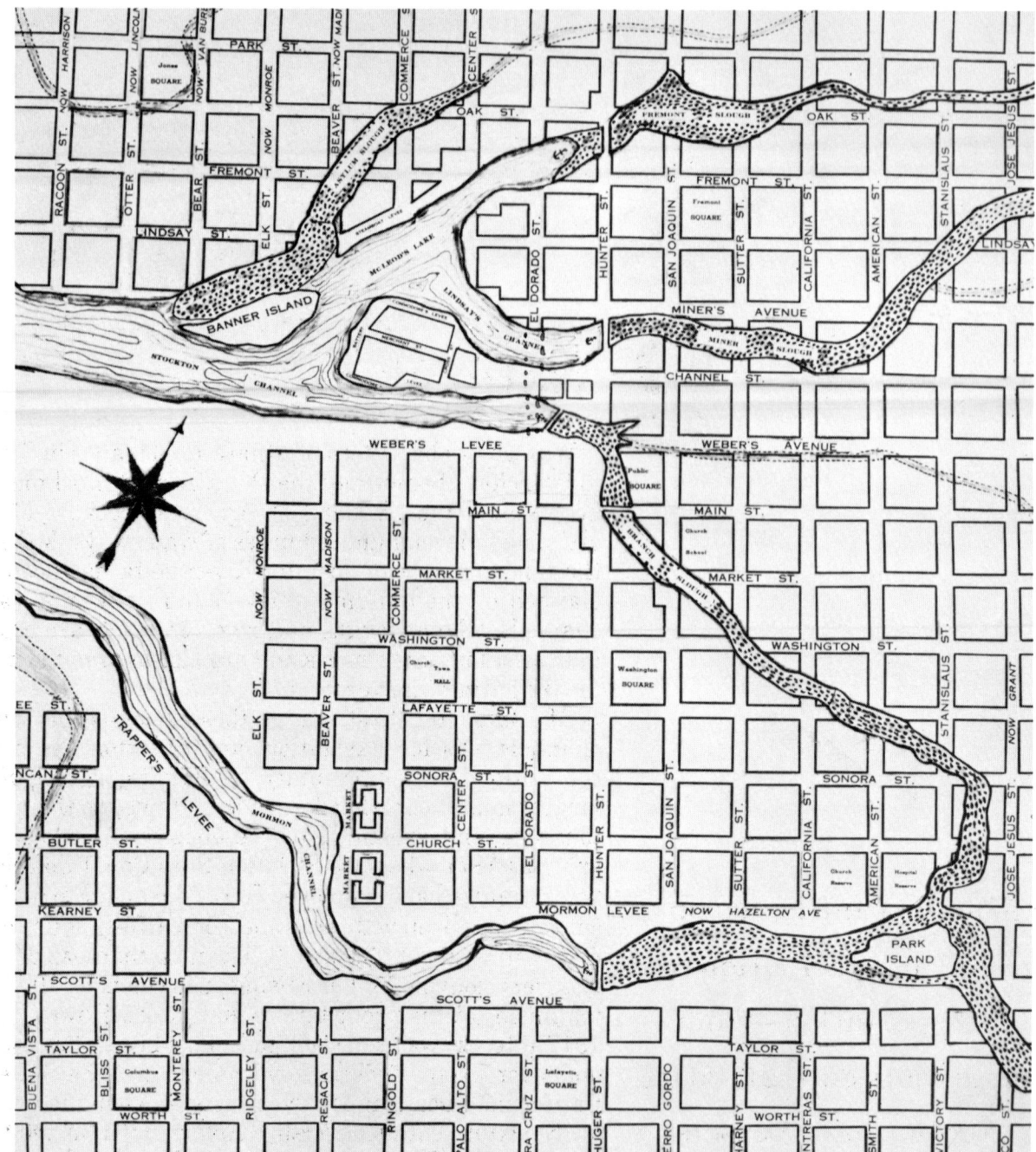

This map, drawn in the 1850s, shows the five sloughs running through the center of Stockton. The only slough that has escaped total filling is Mormon Channel, shown along the bottom of the map.

February 2, 1933, when the *Daisy Gray* was the first deep water ship to make an official call to the Port of Stockton.

Soon ships and cargoes from all parts of the world were arriving at this inland port located over seventy miles from the sea and in the heart of one of the nation's richest agricultural areas. In ten years the total tonnage of the port increased some 236 percent. Among the export items destined for all countries of the world were wine, wheat, barley, large amounts of rice, potatoes, canned goods, iron ore, and agricultural machinery. The Stockton elevator for storing grain at the port is the tallest structure in Stockton, and yet at the peak of harvest season great quantities of grain must be piled in the open. Only Portland, Oregon exceeds the Port of Stockton on the Pacific Coast as a grain terminal. A contract was made with Japanese importers to handle large amounts of iron ore from Utah and Nevada at the ore dock, and a million tons of ore were shipped through the port before the contract was lost in 1967.

By the 1960s thirteen freighters could be berthed at the port at the same time and it was not unusual to see ten or twelve vessels being loaded at the docks. Financially, 1967 was one of its best years. In reporting the banner year, the Port Director stated that over eight million dollars had been paid out in wages at the port. However, the 1970s have brought hard times for various reasons, such as competition with the Port of Sacramento, other means of transportation, the loss of the ore handling contract with Japan, and labor difficulties.

The waterways that have been great assets to Stockton for navigation and recreation have also brought flood problems to Stockton. The maps in this chapter show the possibilities for floods from the various sloughs during the rainy season.

Captain Weber's original land grant map (opposite page one) showing the boundaries of his 48,747-acre "El Rancho del Campo de los Franceses" also indicates the sloughs. Translating the boundaries to known landmarks may be done by starting at a point immediately west of Sharpe Army Depot on the San Joaquin River, following up the river to a line drawn east through the Five Mile House site (Otto's Restaurant now) to Jack Tone Road and then south along a ragged boundary to Roth Road. This area would include the Calaveras River plus a number of sloughs.

The map of the early 1850s shows five sloughs converging to form the Stockton Channel in the heart of Stockton. Most of these waterways have been filled to make streets. Miner Slough became Miner Avenue and Branch Slough became the Plaza or Hunter Square.

As these natural drainage channels were filled in and few other facilities were provided, floods became an annual event during the winter season, inundating all the business section of town for days at a time. The great flood of 1907 brought water depths varying from sixteen inches to four feet all over the city and paralyzed transportation and business. This disaster resulted in plans to build a canal to divert water from Mormon Slough north to the Calaveras River at a point east of West Lane. This Diverting Canal was completed in 1910 and greatly lessened the damage from flood.

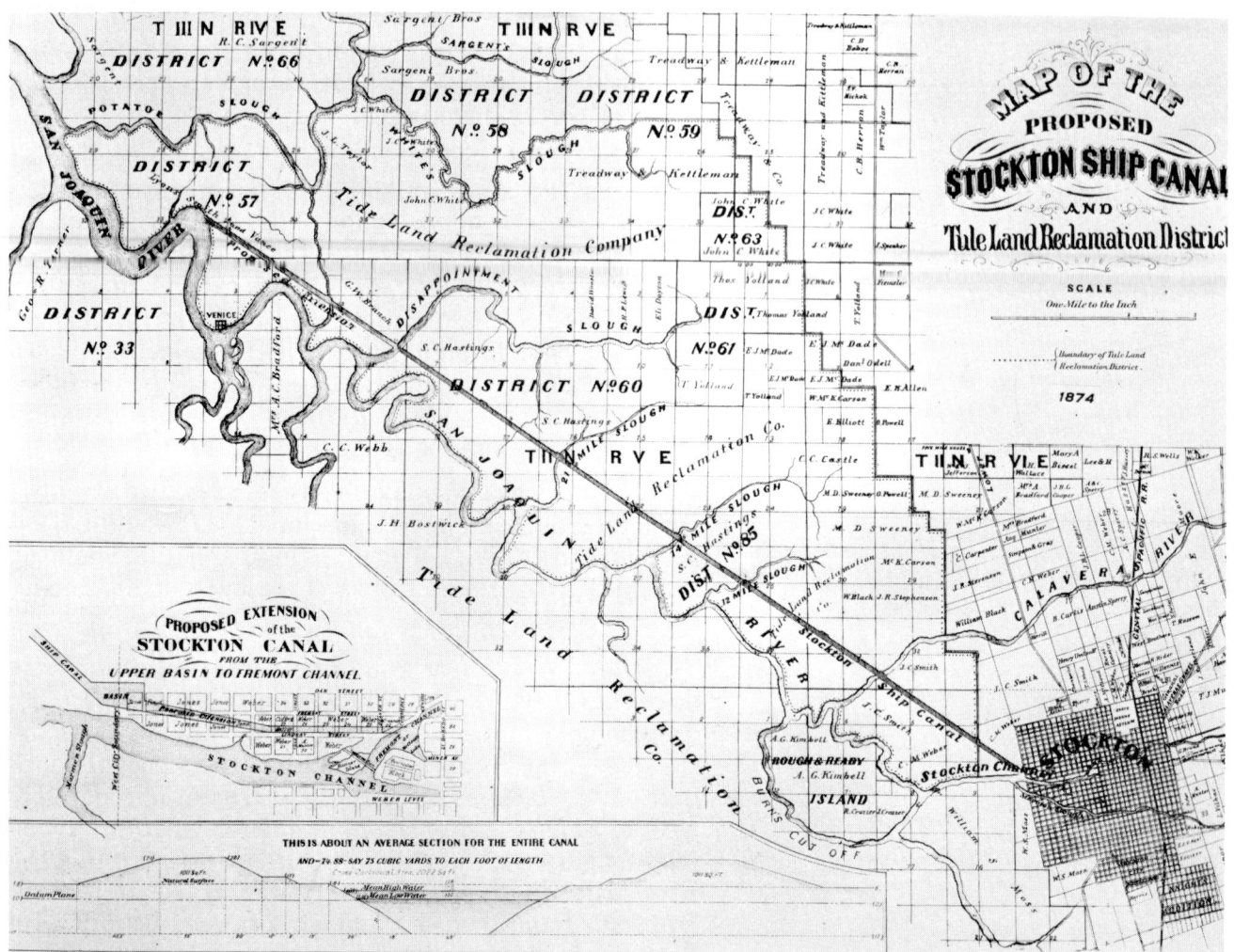

The Hogan Dam, named after Walter Hogan who was City Manager and also an engineer, was built on the Calaveras River near Valley Springs and also controls flood water that could reach Stockton. It was completed in 1930 and soon became a popular recreation area.

In spite of the efforts, the great flood of December 1955 occurred when 7.23 inches of rain fell on Stockton and the entire southern part of the city was flooded. Thousands were evacuated from their homes and transportation was halted in and out of the city.

Since then a number of flood control projects have been completed. From the Old Hogan Dam which had a capacity of 76,000 acre feet to the new Hogan Dam completed in 1963-64 with a capacity of 325,000 acre feet, there has been a vast increase in storage capacity. Because of the "dry years" and additional control measures, Stockton has not had a flood since 1955.

Although this map was drawn in 1874 to show the proposed Stockton ship canal, the same idea was used in dredging for the deep water project starting in 1928. A new straight channel was cut across islands and old channels to provide easy navigation; better use of existing waterways was made than that shown on this map.

From top: Head of navigation, Stockton, 1855. The side-wheeler Eclipse *and the tug boat* Alice *are docked on the south bank of the Stockton channel. Notice the covered wagon alongside of the wooden El Dorado Street bridge.*

Stockton waterfront in 1862. The scene is looking west down the Stockton channel from the head of navigation at the El Dorado Street bridge (foreground). The steamer Sagamore *is moored alongside what is now West Weber Avenue. Weber Point, present location of the Holiday Inn and site of the Weber home, is at the right. On the center left is the main business district of the time along the south bank of the channel. Mt. Diablo is in the background, rising 3,849 feet above sea level.*

Stockton's waterfront, or head of the channel, in the early 1930s. The channel is nearly filled with riverboats. The large billboard in the lower left calls attention to the progress of the Deep Water Project, then 85 percent complete.

Another interesting story concerns the former Sperry Mill, the tall building in the background. The sign atop the old flour mill reads "Liquid Sugar Corp." Many Stocktonians invested money in that fraudulent enterprise that never existed except on paper. A portion of this building was used for many years as the Blake, Moffitt & Towne warehouse, and was demolished early in 1977.

What a thrill it was for Stocktonians to see their dream come true when the Daisy Gray *officially opened the Port of Stockton on February 2, 1933. This view is looking north from a spot where the grain elevators were later erected.*

What an unusual sight to see this large ocean-going vessel, the Golden Gate, *navigating the Stockton channel through the Delta farm lands. The crop in the foreground is milo, grown for cattle feed.*

One of the largest ships to visit the Port of Stockton was the Transeastern. *At 763 feet in length, it was twenty times the size of Captain Weber's first ship, the* Maria, *which first sailed the channel in 1849.*

A 1930 air view of the Delta waterways showing side draft dredges making straight cuts through the old river meandering around Tinsley, Fern, Headreach, and Tule Islands. In the early years side-wheel steamers would navigate a sharp bend by slowing one side wheel and maintaining or increasing the speed of the other paddle wheel. With the larger sternwheelers the sharp bends in the river had to be made wider, and with the coming of deep water vessels most of the bends had to be eliminated altogether. Plans are still being made today for a wider, deeper and more navigable waterway.

Air view of the Port of Stockton about 1940, years before the huge concrete grain elevators were built. The building in the lower left was the location of the cotton compress; with crop changes it is now unused.

Port of Stockton Ore Docks. At one time a million tons of Utah and Nevada iron ore were exported annually to Japan.

When working in tandem, the two great cranes at the Port of Stockton could lift 60,000 pounds. They seem to dwarf the elevators in the background.

In the 1950s and 1960s it was not unusual to see as many as ten or twelve ocean-going vessels tied up at the port at one time. The Stockton Port has berthing accommodations for thirteen ocean-going freighters. The Port has had rough years in the 1970s due to lack of shipping business and labor problems. Several changes in Port Directors have not solved the problems.

The Port of Stockton in the 1960s. Nine ships can be seen docked in the channel and turning basin. The channel is thirty feet deep and 225 feet wide all the way to Suisun Bay. In the 1960s more than 150 truck lines and three major railroads serviced the Port. The port area consists of 485 acres with 257 acres reserved for a partially developed industrial park.

The President Lincoln docked alongside of the $4,500,000 Stockton Elevators. Stockton is the West Coast's second largest grain terminal, next to Portland, Oregon. The head house of the elevators towers 220 feet above the ground and is the tallest structure in the city.

McLeod's Lake, c. 1920. Buildings in the background were on site now occupied by the north side of City Hall.

McLeod's Lake used to be nearly filled with these house boats or "arks" and many men made permanent homes in them. A large portion of McLeod's Lake was filled in during 1947 and that was the end of the arks.

Old Hogan Dam. This flood control dam was completed on the Calaveras River, thirty-five miles east of Stockton, in 1930. It was named for Walter Hogan, popular City Manager.

A new, higher dam, also called Hogan Dam, was built just downstream of the old dam, which was covered when the reservoir was filled. The old dam reappeared during the 1976-1977 drought.

3 Transportation

As explorers and settlers moved west across the continent they used rivers and lakes as highways wherever possible. Even when a river was too small to permit riverboat transportation, its banks provided grass and access to water for the teams and stock. That meant that the first large towns were located on rivers or lakes or were seaports.

In California the only exception to this trend was Los Angeles, which was established some twenty miles inland from a small unimportant harbor at San Pedro.

When Captain Weber first traveled along the edges of the Delta he certainly was aware of the navigable waterways that could be used for transporting supplies by riverboat from San Francisco. Sometimes historians speculate on why he founded his town at the juncture of five sloughs; the obvious answer is that he saw the possibilities of an inland port in the heart of a rich agricultural area served by riverboats and barges. Therefore, historically the most significant means of transportation to Stockton has been shipping on the San Joaquin River. Hundreds of small sailing vessels, barges and paddlewheel riverboats have carried freight and passengers between Stockton and San Francisco. The gold rush in 1848 and 1849 greatly increased the river traffic, and, as eager gold seekers came to Stockton, many of them abandoned their boats there and headed for the Southern Mines. The Stockton Channel became so clogged that Weber ordered the abandoned boats towed to Mormon Slough, stripped of their valuable lumber and burned.

One of the first vessels used on the San Joaquin River was Weber's 38-foot-long two-masted sailing sloop, the *Maria*, which was launched in Oregon City. As it was small it had a draft of only thirty-nine inches. Other riverboats had even shallower drafts and it was claimed, could come in "on the morning dew."

In 1848 Weber loaded the *Maria* with thirteen tons of supplies in San Francisco and landed it at the head of the Stockton Channel. In an 1849 San Francisco news-

Crossroads for agriculture and commerce, by water, rail, air and highway

paper advertisement Weber invited settlers to come to his new community and named several boats that were serving Stockton. He listed the *San Joaquin*, the *Progress*, the *Invincible*, and the brig *Susanne*.

Historians find it impossible to name for sure the first steam powered riverboat to reach Stockton, but George Tinkham, Stockton's first historian, said it was the *Captain Sutter*, a sidewheeler arriving in 1849 under the command of a Captain Warren.

It is claimed that the *Santa Clara*, a side-wheeler built in San Francisco, was the first steamer built on the Pacific coast for use on the San Joaquin River. Captain Warren was behind the construction of the *Santa Clara* and took over command of it. He was a most colorful and capable commander and set a speed record of seven hours between San Francisco and Stockton in 1851 with a small side-wheeler named the *Jenny Lind*.

Traffic developed to the extent that rival companies were contending for the business in "steamboat wars" in 1851-52, but in 1854 the California Steam Navigation Company was organized in San Francisco with a capital stock of two million dollars, and gained control of river transportation by purchasing all river steamers available. Four new boats were put on the Stockton route and the *Julia* and *Amador* were the 'floating palaces' for a number of years. This company operated profitably and efficiently until the Central Pacific Railroad was completed in 1870 creating competition for freight, passengers and mail.

This was the beginning of the eventual elimination of the steamboats from the San Joaquin River. Old-timers still remember the names of some of the famous stern-wheelers such as the *Mary Garratt*, the *T. C. Walker*, the *Captain Weber*, the *J. D. Peters*, and the last and largest, the *Delta King* and *Delta Queen*.

The *King* and *Queen* were palatial stern-wheelers built in Stockton for passenger service and were the last river steamers built in California for this purpose. The hulls were prefabricated in Scotland and brought to Stockton for reassembly and construction of the superstructures. After two and one-half years in the shipyard of the California Navigation and Improvement Company, the twin steamers were completed and dedicated on May 20, 1927. They rarely returned to Stockton as most of their runs were scheduled between San Francisco and Sacramento.

These great riverboats were built too late and couldn't meet the competition of trains, trucks and autos, and were removed from service in 1941. The *Delta Queen* is still operating as an excursion boat on the Mississippi and Ohio Rivers. The hulk of the *Delta King* is anchored at Rio Vista on the Sacramento River.

Another part of the story of transportation in Stockton involved important carriage and wagon-building firms that opened as a result of the need for transporting passengers and freight to the Southern Mines and the Mother Lode. One of the largest freight wagons ever built on the West Coast was built in Stockton.

Stockton has been favored with three major transcontinental railroads and several smaller railroad lines. On August 12, 1869, the little balloon-stacked locomotive "Governor Stanford" pulled the first excursion train into Stockton from Sacramento for a tremendous celebration. This was only three months after the Central Pacific Railroad, owned by the "Big Four," completed the first transcontinental railroad by meeting the tracks of the Union Pacific at Promontory Summit, Utah. An extension of the Central Pacific was completed to Oakland on September 7, giving Stockton access to transcontinental railroad service. However, Stockton was not the division point it might have been because the city council refused to meet the demands of the "Big Four," including a gift of land for a railroad yard at the end of the channel. Lathrop, a few miles south, was established as the division point for trains going south down the valley and those bound for Oakland, and Leland Stanford boasted that Lathrop would become the larger community.

In 1870 a second railroad was begun, the Stockton and Copperopolis Railroad, with a depot on Weber Avenue on the Stockton Channel. This railroad was to haul the rich copper ore from the Copperopolis mines to riverboats at Stockton. It was completed only to Milton, a few miles northwest of Copperopolis, but freight and passengers from the Mother Lode were brought to Stockton via this thirty-mile-long line. It was purchased by Southern Pacific soon after completion.

The Santa Fe Railroad came to Stockton with the purchase in 1898 of the San Francisco and San Joaquin Valley Railroad, which had been built to give competition to the Southern Pacific. The first train from Stockton to Fresno made its run on October 5, 1896. It was completed to Oakland in 1904.

The third major railroad, the Western Pacific line between Salt Lake City and San Francisco, began operation in 1909. These three transcontinental railroads, along with motor vehicles, now gave overwhelming competition to riverboat service and it was gradually discontinued.

Important dates in local automobile history:
- 1907 - First Sheriff's auto
- 1908 - First taxi, Howell Taxi Company
- 1912 - Barney Oldfield at the county racetrack
- 1914 - First state license plates
- 1915 - Enameled plates were yellow on black
- 1920 - Beginning of new license plates every year
- 1922 - Stockton had 7,500 autos
- 1924 - Gas tax 2¢ per gallon

Transportation on the streets of Stockton was provided by horsedrawn streetcars as early as 1875. These were slow one-horse cars, but were better than walking.

Streetcars of the Stockton Electric Railroad began operating on July 15, 1892. All nine of these small ten-horsepower cars were manufactured by the Stockton Combined Harvester and Agricultural Works.

The Southern Pacific Railroad purchased the Stockton Electric Railroad in 1905. The California Traction Co. operated the big red cars to Lodi and Sacramento for years. By 1941 all the electric car service was discontinued and replaced by the motor coaches or buses of the Stockton City Lines.

As autos and highways improved, Stockton, located on the main highways, became a key auto and tourist service center.

One of the famous early pilots, Lincoln Beachy, landed his little biplane on the fairgrounds racetrack in 1914. This was the beginning of the influence of aircraft in Stockton history. Biplanes were soon being used for crop dusting, and the later development of air freight has benefited Stockton in the shipping of the first fruit to eastern markets.

It was not until the 1940s that Stockton began to plan for an adequate municipal airport. Now Stockton and San Joaquin County take pride in the services provided at the Stockton Metropolitan Airport to general aviation and three major airlines, Hughes Airwest, Pacific Southwest Airlines, and United Airlines. In addition to these airlines, fine air taxi services provide charter flights to many smaller airports.

Freight wagon and trailer at El Dorado and Main Streets bound for the waterfront to load supplies for the Southern Mines, c. 1860s. Today there are 125 trucking lines operating in Stockton.

A "Mountain Freighter" built at Stockton in the 1850s. These large wagons could carry as much as 20,000 pounds and were often seen on the road between Stockton and Sonora. There was no seat for the driver and he often rode the wheel horse. Trucking has changed in the 127 years since this wagon was a common sight.

This famous riverboat was the 206-foot-long sternwheeler, J. D. Peters. She was built locally at the Jarvis Shipyards in 1889, and named in honor of a well-known grain merchant and community-minded citizen. The Peters made regular runs between Stockton and San Francisco for nearly fifty years. In the 1920s and early thirties you could board her at the head of the channel at 6:00 P.M. The ticket to San Francisco was one dollar. A berth was a dollar and a fine seven-course dinner in the dining room cost fifty cents. You would be awakened when the steamer docked in San Francisco the following morning.

The J. D. Peters tied up in McLeod's Lake alongside of the Civic Auditorium during the Rotary convention in Stockton in 1925. In those days steamboats would be used as hotels during celebrations and conventions. McLeod's Lake was filled in during 1947 and Fremont Street (center) was continued up to El Dorado Street. Even more important, Center Street was also extended across the former waterway, no longer ending at the Stockton Channel.

A sad sight for old-timers was the J. D. Peters on Mandeville Island. The paddle wheel was used to pump out water when the island was flooded by levee breaks in 1938. It was later used as a bunk house for farm workers. The J. D. Peters burned to the ground in 1965 when it was ignited by sparks from a grass fire.

A favorite riverboat among many Stocktonians was the 200-foot-long, 787-ton T. C. Walker. *It was built in 1885 and was used on the Stockton-San Francisco run into the 1930s. At one time there were as many as ten steamboats and barges running between Stockton and San Francisco.*

The Delta Queen *and* Delta King *under construction on the north bank of the Stockton Channel. They were built by the California Transportation Company and dedicated in Stockton on May 20, 1927. These two sternwheelers were the largest to operate on the San Joaquin and Sacramento Rivers before deep water. The large buildings shown here face North Harrison Street and are part of the Stockton Iron Works where parts of the sister ships were manufactured.*

The Delta Queen *and* Delta King *tied up together on the south bank of the Stockton Channel in 1941 after their Sacramento-San Francisco run was abandoned. These sternwheelers cost nearly one million dollars each and never operated at a profit due to the competition of truck transportation and the automobile.*

A horsecar heading north on El Dorado Street from Main Street. Part of the Holden Drug Store is on the right. This picture was taken in the 1880s.

Horsecar on the Plaza in 1884. Notice the dome of Stockton's first courthouse in the background.

One of the runs of the Big Red Stockton electric railroad was out North California Street to what was considered North Stockton. Seated in the car is Dave Mathews, a city councilman. This car was built in St. Louis in 1906, and had a forty horsepower motor and a capacity of forty passengers. Photo taken in about 1920.

A California Traction Co. car heading out East Weber Avenue eventually reached the Lodi vineyards along Cherokee Lane and Sacramento. The fare was fifty cents. Several of these cars would be put into service to accommodate the large crowds attending the rival football games between Stockton and Lodi High Schools, c. 1920s.

The city leased a number of small streetcars from Southern Pacific. This twenty-eight-passenger, one-man-operated car, with a twenty-five horsepower engine, is shown at Weber Avenue and California Street in the late 1930s. It was typical of the last streetcars to operate in Stockton. All streetcar operations ceased in September 1941. This car was known as a Birney type and was built in St. Louis in 1921.

THE AUTO CAME...
A 1922 crash between representatives of the two big auto rivals: Chevrolet and Ford (the "Tin Lizzie"). The bout appears to have ended in a draw.

The Tucker automobile, "the car to revolutionize all cars," on display at the Stockton Armory in 1948. Many Stocktonians made a bad investment in this venture. Several models were made, so that stock could be sold, but the auto were never put into production.

Mr. and Mrs. John Nagel with their 1959 "his and hers" Edsel cars, in front of their Stockton home.

34

The Central Pacific locomotive pulling the first train into Stockton in August 1869 was the "Governor Stanford," named for one of the Big Four owners of the Central Pacific Railroad. The little engine has been preserved and will be in the State Railroad Museum in Sacramento.

The Central Pacific Railroad depot about 1869. Located on Sacramento Street between Market and Washington Streets, it later became the Southern Pacific depot.

The railroad station and dining room at Lathrop as it appeared in 1889 when David S. Terry, a Stockton attorney, was shot and killed by Supreme Court Justice Stephen Field's body guard, David Neagle.

35

The Stockton and Copperopolis Railroad Depot located along the Stockton Channel near Center Street. It was the first railroad to tap the head of navigation. Tracks extended east through the city along Weber Avenue, into the county to Peters and then to Milton in the foothills. There was also a branch line to Oakdale.

This scene was taken about 1895. A Southern Pacific passenger train is traveling east on Weber Avenue at San Joaquin Street on the old Stockton and Copperopolis R.R. tracks. The Stockton Channel can be seen in the background. The Tretheway Block, the tallest building facing Weber Avenue, is still standing today.

The Southern Pacific Railroad Station at Sacramento Street between Main Street and Weber Avenue, in 1909. In 1930 the Southern Pacific built a new brick station a block north of the old depot. The old building was torn down in the 1950s.

For years the only locomotive on the Stockton Terminal and Eastern was Engine #1, an antique that first saw service on the Central Pacific. Service started on this line September 5, 1910 and it wasn't long before it had a nickname, "Slow, Tired and Easy." The company is still in business and is more active today then ever.

The Santa Fe Depot, at 735 South San Joaquin Street since 1900. The oldest railroad station in Stockton, it still serves its original purpose as a passenger depot. AMTRAK trains stop daily.

One of the last Southern Pacific "iron horses" through Stockton before steam locomotives were replaced by diesel engines.

Western Pacific's "California Zephyr" passenger train makes its last appearance at the Stockton depot March 21, 1970.

After completion in late 1909, the Western Pacific operated freight trains only until passenger service was initiated in August 1910. The depot was closed in 1970 and later became headquarters for the Stockton Police Department Youth Activities.

Lincoln Beachy was in Stockton with his biplane for an exhibition at the County Fairgrounds in 1914.

The Stockton Metropolitan Airport, located southeast of Stockton, is operated by the San Joaquin County government. A twenty-three-member staff headed by airport manager Ralph Tonseth administers the facility. Its 8,500-foot jet runway gives San Joaquin County access to some of the fastest modes of air service for passengers, freight and mail. During 1976, 220,327 passengers either boarded or arrived here, an increase of 25,000 over the previous year. It is a major alternate terminal when bad weather closes San Francisco and Bay Area airports. In 1916 there was an airfield just north of American Legion Park. For a short time starting in 1914, the County Fairgrounds race track was used as an airstrip. A small field with one adobe hangar was taken over in 1940 by the U.S. Army Air Force to become the Air Forces Advanced Training School at Stockton Field. It was a major training base throughout World War II. The site is now part of the Stockton Metropolitan Airport. Many of the buildings constructed early in the war, seen on the lower right, were torn down or moved away in 1975.

The Stockton Metropolitan Airport terminal houses administrative offices for three major airlines, a boarding lobby, restaurant, lounge and banquet room. For a time, the airport was used by airlines from all over the world as a training field for their new pilots. It was not unusual to see eight or nine jets practicing takeoffs and landings. The pilot training has been reduced since some airlines started simulation training at the San Francisco Airport. (Note the Japan Air Line jet over the airport building.)

4 Business and Commerce

Supply and business center in Gold Rush days—world marketplace today

A brief look at the history of Stockton's business and industry reveals the influence of its location and environment on the development of the economic life of the community. Two things appealed to Captain Weber when he obtained the Mexican land grant in 1844. He was impressed with the richness of the land, with the great oak forest and the tall, rank grass that covered the plains, and had visions of a great agricultural community. He also realized that the San Joaquin River and its tributary channels were ideally situated for commerce and shipping and could play a role in the beginning of his settlement. These assets were enough for him to resolve that he would return and establish a city at the head of year-round navigation on the San Joaquin River.

He couldn't even have imagined the other great development that was so important: the discovery of gold in the foothills of the Sierra Nevada Mountains. This discovery by James Marshall in January 1848 on the American River came at a very strategic time for Weber in his efforts to attract settlers to his new community. Stockton now became a supply base for the first mines in what are called the Southern Mines, a major portion of the Mother Lode Country. One author has dramatically characterized Stockton's history under the title of "Gold, Grain and the River." It is an oversimplification, of course, of the business history of Stockton, but these were the main elements. As the years passed a great and intricate system of businesses and industries developed.

In the 1850s, as there was a great need for transportation to the mines by wagons and stagecoaches, carriage and wagon manufacturers became established in Stockton. One of the earliest was William P. Miller, later followed by the immensely successful M. P. Henderson, who built wagons, drays, buckboards and vehicles of every description and shipped these products everywhere by river steamer. Hickinbotham Brothers was not only a well-known supplier of carriage and wagon

Taken in 1910, this is the only known picture ever taken of the Union Safe Deposit Bank, which was started by E. C. Stewart in 1897 at 30 North San Joaquin Street. The bank moved to 327 East Main Street in 1923 and now has four locations. The Stewart family is still in the business, E. C. Stewart having been followed by his son, C. E., and he by his son, D. R. Stewart.

327 East Main Street, Downtown Stockton

1340 North El Dorado Street, Stockton

5555 North Pershing Avenue, North Stockton

East Main & North Walnut Streets, Lockeford

parts, but also a hardware dealer. The Stockton Iron Works is famous for the invention of a clam shell dredging bucket which was important in reclaiming the Delta and keeping open shipping channels.

The communities developed by the gold mining in the Mother Lode required food and goods of all kinds, and Stockton became a center of supply of large amounts of agricultural produce. The Mormons were the first to grow wheat in the Ripon area in the 1840s. By the middle 1850s enough wheat was grown to ship some to San Francisco. By the 1880s grain farming made San Joaquin County one of the major producers in the United States, and grain dealers, such as F. E. Ferrell and Company and J. D. Peters, did a large business. The Sperry Flour Mills and others were established to process the wheat.

After the 1890s other types of agriculture became important, especially with the development of irrigation, and Stockton became a center for the processing and shipping of large amounts of fruit, nuts, and vegetable products. As San Joaquin County developed into the fifth or sixth richest agricultural county in the nation, food processing became very important and several canneries opened in and around the community. One of the most dramatic and significant of these was Tillie Lewis Foods, Inc., which started in 1935.

Many important mechanical and technical inventions advancing agriculture were born in Stockton, such as the combined harvester for grain, the Stockton gang plow, and the Caterpillar track-type tractor. The Holt Manufacturing Company of Stockton became world famous for its products. The Samson Iron Works also assembled a tractor used in agriculture. All development of mining and agricultural business was largely dependent upon shipping on the river. Riverboats providing low freight and passenger rates contributed to making Stockton a major river port. Some figures from the middle 1880s indicate the extent of the shipping activity. It was claimed that eighteen steamboats and sixteen barges operating out of the port carried 40,000 passengers and 50,000 tons of freight between Stockton and San Francisco in 1886.

All this shipping activity meant financing and banks, and Stockton business attracted the best. The T. Robinson Bours Bank was one of the fine early banks. Organized in 1852, it later became the San Joaquin Valley Bank. The Stockton Savings and Loan Society was chartered in 1867 and became the Bank of Stockton in 1958. The Bank of Italy, later the Bank of America with five sites in various parts of Stockton, has been of great importance to the financial and business life of the area.

Travelers to Stockton, coming first by riverboat and later by three transcontinental railroads, required hotels and restaurants. One of the first major hotels was the St. Charles or Stockton House, located near the head of the Stockton Channel, but in time the Yosemite House and the Imperial Hotel became the leaders in providing accommodations. Probably the most significant hotel of all was the Hotel Stockton, completed in 1910 at the head of the channel in beautiful Mission Revival style architecture. It was the "Grand Hotel" for Stockton until auto transportation brought about competing motels.

Restaurants were also important and many old-timers remember On Lock Sam's in the heart of Chinatown, Hart's Cafeteria on Main Street, and Johnnie's Waffle Shop, where the coffee was free and liberally provided.

The El Dorado Brewing Company provided famous Valley Brew Beer to the restaurants and saloons, not only in Stockton, but all over Central California.

M. P. Henderson and Son, 609 East Main Street, was established in 1869. They were particularly famous for stagecoaches, but built vehicles of every description. Their products were widely sold on the West Coast. This view was taken about 1890.

William P. Miller, carriage manufacturer in Stockton since 1852, built this plant on the southwest corner of Channel and California Streets in 1893. Stockton-made wagons were found everywhere in the state.

The Pacific Tannery covered over a square block at El Dorado and Oak Streets and operated from 1856 to 1926. Two buildings from the old plant are still standing. The oldest, occupied by Mr. D's Pizzaria, was built in 1871 and is now one of the nearly twenty local historical landmark buildings and sites designated by the Stockton Cultural Heritage Board and the City Council.

The Avenue Stable was on Weber Avenue between California and American Streets. Patrick Fee was the proprietor.

Con Harkins Blacksmith Shop was located on North California Street. Tom Powers is holding the horse and to the right of Powers is the proprietor, Con Harkins. The letter carrier is William Elsom, Stockton's first mail carrier. Standing to the left of the doorway is the old-time blacksmith, Louis Armbrust.

The California Paper Company was established on the Mormon Channel in 1877. It was a unique industry—a pioneer recycling plant. The company produced newsprint and wrapping paper from rags, old paper, and straw, for wide use on the West Coast.

F. E. Ferrell and Company at 305 South California Street. Notice the hard rubber tires on the delivery truck. Ferrell employed a large staff with whom he was popular.

Yolland Materials Company was founded in 1895 by Charles W. Yolland. The company delivered ice, coal, wood, and aggregate to its customers. It is still in business today at 830 South California Street.

Samson Iron Works was first started about 1899 on the southeast corner of California and Washington Streets. Shortly thereafter the company moved to the corner of Jefferson and Aurora Streets. They assembled round-wheeled Samson Tractors featuring the sieve-grip tread. The company later became a division of General Motors.

Grain dealer J. D. Peters had his office on Channel Street between Center and El Dorado Streets next to the old Weber Fire House. Mr. Peters was an outstanding community leader. The steamboat J. D. Peters, which ran on the river until 1938, was named in his honor and the little town of Peters, near Linden, was named after him. He was also elected Grand Marshal of the 1876 Centennial celebration in Stockton. Peters was also president of the California Navigation and Improvement Company. This picture was taken about 1890. Notice the sign "Buhach Depot." Buhach was grown on land Peters owned in Merced County, ground into a powder and used for controlling insect pests in many households.

In 1900 the Stockton Iron Works was located at 25 North California Street and C. G. Hyatt was president. A few years later the company moved to the north bank of the Stockton Channel. They made parts for the famous *Delta King* and *Delta Queen* riverboats, but were best known for developing the clam shell dredging bucket which was so important in reclamation work in the Delta.

These coal bunkers, used to supply riverboats with freight and fuel, were located along the south bank of the Stockton Channel. The Stockton Alameda and San Joaquin Railroad Company transported coal from the Tesla Coal Mines in Corral Hollow, west of Tracy, to Stockton. The mines were closed in 1910 and the bunkers were abandoned soon afterward.

Interior view of the Hammond and Yardley Grocery Store at 233 East Weber Avenue c. 1910. This store provided choice groceries, lime, cement, plaster, pure paints, oils, and builders' hardware. To see the store from the outside, as it looked on July 4, 1876, turn to page 70.

M. Orsi's Grocery and fruit and vegetable stand was located at 247 South California Street about 1910.

The Yosemite Cash Grocery Store was located on the northeast corner of San Joaquin Street and Weber Avenue, the location today of the Belding Building. At upper left is the old Columbia House Hotel, at Channel and San Joaquin Streets. In the background can be seen the county jail and the spires of the Methodist Church. At the far right is the spire of the First Congregational Church. This photograph was taken in about 1900.

McCormack Bros. Wholesale and Retail Meat Market at Main and Center Streets about 1910. Butchers hung the meat out in front of the store, before the days of laws of sanitation.

The Wagner Meat Company, which did both wholesale and retail business, was located at 543 East Weber Avenue. The president was J. K. Wagner and the vice president was George Devaney. Notice that the truck has just one headlamp.

The Family Grocery Store was located on the northwest corner of Main and Center Streets. It was run by Alexander and Houston Black. The family later operated grocery stores all over the Central Valley with about five stores in Stockton. All old-timers will remember the Black Grocery Stores.

Sunset Macaroni Factory delivery wagon, decorated for a 1915 parade to display the various kinds of pasta produced by the company. The pasta had to be displayed freshly made because upon drying it would break up. The wagon had a tree limb on top with spaghetti hanging on the branches and a sign that read, "In Stockton Macaroni grows on trees." When brothers Dave and Frank Stagnaro started the business in 1909 at 428 South American Street it would take one man one hour to make a hundred pounds of macaroni. Today Frank Stagnaro's grandson operates the business at the same location, and can produce 1,200 pounds of macaroni in one hour by pressing a button.

Stockton's finest banking institution, the T. Robinson Bours Bank, was organized in 1852. Bours and Company was reorganized in 1868 as the San Joaquin Valley Bank with C. B. Claiborn as president. In 1917 both banks were taken over by the Bank of Italy. Wells Fargo and Company, destined to become the largest express company, was organized in 1852 and opened its first Stockton office in 1853 at Center Street between Main and Levee (now West Weber), shown here.

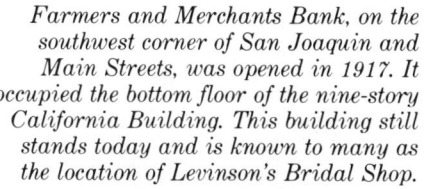

The Bank of Italy was near the northwest corner of Main and Hunter Streets when this photo was taken in the early twenties. It was moved from this location to the former Commercial Bank building on the northwest corner of Main and Sutter Streets, remodeled following a fire in 1923. It became the main branch of the Bank of America, now at Weber Avenue and El Dorado Street. The once familiar Mail Fountain appears on the right. This public drinking fountain was built in 1891 from funds collected from civic-minded citizens by the Stockton Mail newspaper.

Farmers and Merchants Bank, on the southwest corner of San Joaquin and Main Streets, was opened in 1917. It occupied the bottom floor of the nine-story California Building. This building still stands today and is known to many as the location of Levinson's Bridal Shop.

The Stockton Savings and Loan Society Building at San Joaquin and Main Streets was completed in 1908 and still serves as a bank today. (See the same intersection as it looked in 1965, on page 14.) This institution was started in 1867 and was located on the southwest corner of Main and Hunter Streets. Now the Bank of Stockton, it is the second bank chartered and the second oldest bank in California operating under its original charter. During its first year in business, Dr. J. M. Kelsey was president and B. Bours was a major stockholder. The name was changed to Stockton Savings and Loan Bank in 1919 and to its present name, Bank of Stockton, in 1958. The bank now has two other locations, at Miner Avenue and San Joaquin and at Benjamin Holt and Pacific Avenue.

The St. Charles Hotel, originally the Stockton House, was built in 1849. It was the first good hotel in the city and was located on Bridge Street opposite the head of the Channel. The grand opening of the $75,000 hostelry was held on March 23, 1850; a few years later it became the St. Charles.

The Yosemite House at 337 East Main Street was considered Stockton's finest hotel before the turn of the century. It had several horsedrawn omnibuses to call for guests at the railroad depot. Ulysses S. Grant was a guest at this hotel in 1880 while on a tour of Central California and the Mother Lode. The Yosemite House was built in 1869 for $40,000, and had 200 rooms. The dining room seated 110 people. The front of the building measured 102 feet across. The hotel later became a rooming house, and in the early twenties it burned down. (Flaws in photograph are due to its age and condition.)

The Imperial Hotel, 904 East Main Street, was built in 1897 at a cost of $40,000 by the Rothenbush family of brewery fame. It was the first hotel in Stockton to have hot and cold water in every room. It catered mostly to traveling men as it was located close to the railroad depots. Buses picked up guests at all the depots, including the Santa Fe out on South San Joaquin Street. After a fire destroyed the upper floors in the late 1940s, the hotel went out of business. The main floor is still standing today. Other early day hotels were the Columbia House, Grand Central, Commercial, the Weber, United States Hotel, and the Russ House, among others.

The Lincoln Hotel at 118 South El Dorado Street was considered one of Stockton's finest when it opened in 1919. The 20-30 Club and other service clubs met there for luncheons and club meetings for many years. As it was located in what became "skid row," the hotel eventually became a rooming house for gamblers and prostitutes. During its last years it operated as a workingman's hotel. It was torn down in 1963.

The lobby of the Hotel Stockton with its Indian motif fireplace. The hotel closed in 1960, but had enjoyed a profitable business until parking became a problem and motels were built all around the city.

The Hotel Stockton at 133 East Weber Avenue at El Dorado Street was opened in 1910. The roof garden was added two years later. It featured fine dining rooms and a music gallery and was a popular spot for dining and dancing and watching the sun go down over the Stockton Channel. The hotel had five stories and 252 rooms. Over 200 rooms had connecting bathrooms. Rooms were $1.00 a day without bath and $2.00 with. Its grand opening featured Andrew Blossom's orchestra with Frank Thornton Smith as the vocalist. Although the hotel closed in November 1960, Jacob Fetzer continued to operate the restaurant and bar and called it Webb's at the Stockton. The building was used as a temporary courthouse while the new County Courthouse was being completed. It now houses the County Welfare Department and other offices. It was designated as an official local landmark by the Stockton Cultural Heritage Board, as it is considered one of the finest examples of Mission Revival architecture in California.

The Hotel Wolf at 409 East Market Street was opened in 1924. It had a beautiful Roof Garden for dining and was considered Stockton's finest hotel, next to the Hotel Stockton. It is now operated as a senior citizens' hotel.

The Hotel Clark was built in 1911 on the southeast corner of Market and Sutter Streets. Most of the large older hotels in Stockton, including this one, have been converted into inexpensive living quarters for senior citizens.

Here is the beautiful lobby of the Hotel Clark, now much changed. The top three hotels in Stockton during the early decades of the 20th century were the Stockton, the Wolf, and the Clark. The Clark also had a lovely dining room where dinner dances were held nightly.

The Royal Shaving Parlor was located at 39 North Hunter Street on the Plaza from 1896 to 1899. In those days most of the patrons had their own shaving mugs which were kept in the shop. The Royal also featured the Royal Bath where for an extra quarter you would be given a towel and a hot tub. Notice the poster ads on the ceiling. While you were being shaved you could look at the commercials—sort of a forerunner to television.

The Tillie Lewis Stockton plant covers over 180 acres and has its own can-making plant. Tillie Lewis Foods is Stockton's largest cannery, turning out six million cases of various products each year. Tillie Lewis started the cannery business in 1935 and was soon known as the "Tomato Queen." She started the company with a few pounds of Pomodoro seed (the pear-shaped tomato) and a ton of faith. She died in 1977 at the age of 75, shortly after a speaking engagement. The Tillie Lewis Theatre at Delta College was named in her honor.

The Stockton Dry Goods Company was founded by A. B. Cohn in 1914. On the twenty-first anniversary of the store's opening a plaque was placed in the sidewalk on the northeast corner of Main and American Streets by friends and employees. It is still in place today.

This photograph from the 1930s shows a huge crowd waiting in the rain for a drawing for some long-forgotten prize. The building was later taken over by Breuner's. It still stands today.

This building on the southeast corner of Main and San Joaquin Streets housed the Hale Department Store in 1900. It later became Weinstock Lubin, then Weinstock Hale, and still later Smith and Lang. After the building was destroyed by fire in 1956 the store was closed and Weinstocks moved to North Stockton. Smith and Lang rebuilt on the site and their former store is now new quarters for the County Assessor.

The El Dorado Brewery was operated by the Rothenbush family for over 100 years. They produced the famous Valley Brew Beer that was distributed all over Central California. This 1893 view shows the buildings on American between Oak and Park Streets. The plant closed in 1955 and today the site is a large retirement and apartment complex.

The Coney Island Chili Parlor was at 825 East Main Street from 1922 to 1924. Shown above from left to right are: Tom Pappas, Tom Karras, Kris Speras, Spiro Rizo, Nick Sperry (proprietor), Nick Tadernarakis, Gus Lakas, and Tom Apos. There were several other Coney Island Restaurants operating in Stockton from the 1920s through the 1940s.

"Harts Lunch" at 435 East Main Street was opened in 1919. This is one of Stockton's best-remembered cafeterias and it was here that everyone met after a night on the town. Harts Lunch was closed in the late 1940s and moved to South Sutter Street where it was operated as the Gold Rush Restaurant. Other noted restaurants in Stockton over the years were Zuzallo's, Maddens, Delmonico's, the Arlington, and Campe's.

Johnnie's Waffle Shop on the northwest corner of Market and Sutter Streets, and a small portrait insert of Johnnie himself. This was a popular restaurant in the 1930s and '40s. It had a long counter with several self-contained coffee percolators brewing all the time. In the cold winter months you could smell the coffee long before you arrived at the shop. Johnnie's Waffle Shop is still in business today on South Wilson Way.

A new sign was apparently put up not long after this picture was taken. See page 56.

The On Lock Sam Chinese restaurant was located in the heart of Stockton's Chinatown from 1895 to 1966 and will be remembered by many old-timers. In 1966 the restaurant moved to a palatial new building at 333 South Sutter Street, where it is still in operation.

In 1906, after the San Francisco earthquake, 5,000 Chinese moved to Stockton. By 1921 the number dwindled to 1,071, but just a few years later there were about 3,000. Half of them were farmers or farm workers. Stockton still has a sizeable Chinese community.

Otto's Five Mile House, Pacific Avenue and Hammer Lane. Most local people are acquainted with Otto's of today, a fine gourmet restaurant. This is how it looked in 1932 with Mr. Otto standing in front wearing an apron.

Newby's Drive Inn on East Harding Way and Palm Street served outstanding barbecued beef and pork sandwiches. Other drive-ins operating in the 1940s in Stockton were: the Parrot, on Wilson Way; the Bob In, at El Dorado and Rose Streets; Dick's Drive In, Harding Way and West Lane; and the Miracle Drive In, on Pacific and Castle Streets. At those drive-ins cute young girls, called carhops, wore special uniforms and came out to wait on customers, who stayed in their cars. Now the customer either gets out of the car and goes inside, or drives past a speaker to give the order and then to a window to pick it up.

5 Buildings

The history of a community can almost be told in terms of the important buildings that have been erected over the years, especially the public and semi-public buildings. This history is written in bricks, stones and building materials with the labor, skill and pride of people in the community.

Stockton has been fortunate that its founder, Captain Weber, was so proud of his community and encouraged fine public buildings through donations of land and personal finances.

One of the first important public buildings was the Corinthian Building built in 1850. Located at the head of the Stockton Channel, it was Stockton's first large building and was used for courtrooms, city offices and many other purposes. It also had a large auditorium which could be used for entertainment and assemblies. Many traveling groups of entertainers performed there.

Stockton became a shipping center for grain by 1860 and the first Agricultural Society was organized in 1855. The city's position as an agricultural center had its influence on large buildings. The California State Fair can be traced back to 1854 and 1855 when legislation was passed to hold it alternately in San Francisco, Sacramento, Stockton and Marysville. The State Fair was held in Stockton in 1857 in a large exhibit tent erected on Hunter Square, as this was the popular place for festivals and was in the heart of the city.

Just a few years later the district fair concept was successfully organized by the San Joaquin Valley Agricultural Association. For years Erastus Holden was president of this organization which held the fair for eight counties in the valley. The county courthouse had been used at "fair time" to show some farm production, but in August 1860 an additional pavilion made of a wooden frame covered by canvas was erected in the plaza. On the last night of the fair a Grand Ball was held to raise funds for construction of a permanent building. A location was obtained on San Joaquin Street across from the courthouse, between Main Street

Framework of a city's life

and Weber Avenue. The Agricultural Hall was completed by 1862 and for several years was an important community center. However, the Agricultural Association ran into financial difficulties and in 1866 this hall was sold to the Methodists for a church building.

The exhibits at the annual fair were held in tents or temporary buildings for several years. In 1880, under the leadership of L. U. Shippee, the Agricultural Association launched a campaign to raise funds for a large permanent hall. In 1885 Washington Square, across from old St. Mary's Catholic Church, was obtained and Stockton's first great auditorium was erected. It was a large wooden building erected in the form of a cross and was known as the Agricultural Pavilion. It was opened on September 15, 1888, with over four thousand people attending the ceremonies and viewing the exhibits. This grand building and show place served well as the community hall until one hot, dry Sunday in 1902 when fire broke out, and in spite of the efforts of the firemen, it burned to the ground in a spectacular blaze. Its site reverted to park purposes for seventy years, until Washington Park was destroyed for construction of the Crosstown Freeway.

It was not until 1926 that Stockton replaced the Pavilion with a large community auditorium. Sentiment had grown to construct a suitable memorial to the young men of Stockton who had given their lives for their country in World War I, and as the Masonic Temple and the theaters were not suitable for large crowds, it was decided to construct the Civic Memorial Auditorium in the planned Civic Center at Fremont and Center Streets. A bond issue was passed for construction of the $687,000 auditorium in 1925. The building was dedicated in November 1926 and has been the heart of Stockton's cultural and recreational activities ever since, also helping make Stockton a desirable convention city.

Two fraternal organizations, the Odd Fellows and the Masons, have erected significant buildings that have served community needs as well as their own. The Odd Fellows constructed their large building on Hunter Square in 1865. The ground floor of the three-story building was used for business. However, it was the large and beautiful Masonic Temple built in 1883 at the head of the channel that contributed most to Stockton community life. The top floor was used as a gymnasium, auditorium, and for dinners and dances. By 1921 the Masons needed a new hall and the present Temple was constructed at Market and Sutter Streets.

The Corinthian Building was completed in September of 1850, near the location of the State of California building today on Channel Street just west of El Dorado. The wooden building was built by Captain Weber and R. P. Hammond and was originally three stories tall. It housed a courtroom, printing office, church, customs office, theater, and a number of private lodgings and offices. Mr. Hammond, an engineer, was hired by Weber to survey the streets of Stockton, and helped in naming them.

Stockton gained a nickname, "The Brick City," because of the number of these early brick buildings, constructed to replace the wooden ones which were so easily destroyed by fire.

Stockton has been fortunate in having a good free public library since Dr. William Hazelton, a dentist and schoolteacher, left his fortune to the city for that purpose in 1895. The Hazelton Library was a beautiful building, veneered with marble and adorned with six marble columns. By the 1950s its location on Market and Hunter Streets had become a part of "Skid Row" and the overcrowded building was deteriorating. Efforts to finance a new library to be located at Oak and El Dorado Streets were finally achieved and in August 1964 Stockton's great new library opened as a part of the beautiful Civic Center.

Another important building and cultural institution is the Pioneer Museum and Haggin Galleries, opened in Victory Park during 1931. This institution devotes 38,000 square feet of space to important collections of nineteenth century American and French art as well as California and local history. A recent addition contains the Holt Memorial Hall, an exhibit on important local industries. It contains Benjamin Holt's experimental shop, a Stockton-built Caterpillar track-type tractor and a 1904 Haines-Houser combined harvester, the oldest on display outside the Smithsonian Institution. This museum offers many temporary shows each year on art and history, in addition to permanent displays. Some operating funds are provided by the city and county, but most are derived from the endowment income of this private, nonprofit institution. Nearly 60,000 visitors, including many school children who are given guided tours, visit this outstanding museum each year.

The three-story Odd Fellows Hall, built in 1865, measured 67 by 95 feet and cost $46,000. It was located on the southeast corner of Main and Hunter Streets. The top two floors were used for the lodge activities, but the street level was rented to businesses. C. O. Burton was president of the lodge at the time the hall was built.

The Masonic Temple at El Dorado and Channel Streets was built in 1883 and razed in 1931. The street level was used for businesses and the Post Office. On the second floor were the lodge rooms. The top floor was used as an auditorium and for dinner dances. The above scene also shows a barge unloading bricks at the head of the Stockton Channel. Stockton was once called "The Brick City."

The San Joaquin Valley Agricultural Society Pavilion was opened on September 15, 1888. Four thousand people heard the dedication speeches and viewed the exhibits. The wooden building, constructed in the shape of a cross, cost $50,000 and had 38,000 square feet of floor space. It was the largest building in Stockton for many years and covered the entire block bounded by Hunter, Washington, San Joaquin, and Lafayette Streets. It burned to the ground in the early evening of September 28, 1902. See picture on page 84.

The Hazelton Library on the northeast corner of Market and Hunter Streets. Stockton's first public library was started by Frank Stewart in 1889, just south of the Central Fire Station. In 1895 William Hazelton willed $75,000 for the Hazelton Library, which was built at the same location. It served for almost seventy years, until the new library was built at Oak and El Dorado Streets in 1964.

When the old library was demolished the eight Ionic style marble columns were moved to the University of the Pacific campus where they were erected at the south side of Knoles Hall, forming a lovely courtyard.

To the left in the picture can be seen the old clock tower that housed the original clockworks and bell used in the first courthouse. Both were placed atop the Central Fire Station.

Children's Home at 430 North Pilgrim Street. The stately brick building has housed almost 2,000 youngsters since it was built in 1912. The Children's Home was first opened in 1880 at the southeast corner of Lafayette and Church Streets. A new building planned for 1978 will be a one-story facility at Pilgrim and Lindsay Streets, next to the existing home, and will cost $450,000.

The Stockton Golf and Country Club of 1925 was located in the same place as the present one. The club is along the Stockton Channel about three miles west of the city at the end of Country Club Boulevard. The timber structure in the background is part of a dredge used for levee maintenance.

The present Masonic Temple Building is on the southwest corner of Market and Sutter Streets. The ground breaking ceremony on August 6, 1921 started with a parade from the old building on El Dorado Street to the new site. The building was completed in 1922 and is still in use today. The elaborate brick building at the left is the Henery Apartments, built about 1914 and also still standing.

The Stockton Memorial Civic Auditorium was dedicated on Armistice Day 1926 as a memorial to the American soldiers of Stockton who lost their lives in World War I. There is a golden bear on each side of the entrance, lending a bit of California history to the appearance of the building. The above picture is framed through the Civic Center fountain and was made with infrared film to give the illusion of being taken at night.

The Stockton-San Joaquin County Library is a part of the Civic Center complex and was opened August 24, 1964, costing $1,700,000. The library features an outdoor pool with fountains and landscaped reading patios and has become a showplace of the city. It contains 500,000 pieces of printed material, including 300,000 books. The children's department contains 19,000 volumes. Bookmobiles extend the library's service throughout the county.

The Pioneer Museum and Haggin Galleries located at Pershing and Rose Streets is open free to the public. Among the most popular exhibits are the nineteenth century French Academic and Salon paintings by Bougeureau and Vibert; the works of Albert Bierstadt, a well-known nineteenth century American landscape painter; an Egyptian mummy; period shop settings; a fine California Indian basket collection; historical vehicles; and the newly opened Holt Memorial Hall honoring local industry. (Photograph courtesy of Pioneer Museum)

6 Government, Politicians and Patriotism

During the gold rush era, when would-be miners of all types were streaming through Stockton, government consisted of remnants of the Spanish-Mexican system, as typified by the alcalde, or mayor, with some military influence because of the United States military governors and, finally, vigilante "justice," when conditions became intolerable.

The first government official in Stockton was Alcalde George Gordon Belt, in 1848. How he obtained his position is uncertain.

On November 13, 1849, Belt called for an election to choose a town council of seven members. This council passed ordinances and considered itself a legal municipal government. The members began to obligate the government financially until they learned they could not collect taxes and were themselves liable for the debts contracted. They quickly ceased operations and Alcalde Belt was left with the responsibility of enforcing the ordinances.

In November 1849, a state constitution was adopted that had been written at Monterey, and state government was established in December 1849, with the inauguration of Governor Peter Burnett and the convening of the first elected state legislature.

California's first twenty-seven counties were created on February 18, 1850 by the legislature, and San Joaquin County was one of them. An election was held on April 1, 1850 to choose county officials who were sworn in on April 3. Benjamin Williams was the first county judge and Dr. R. Porter Ashe was elected sheriff.

The Court of Sessions was selected and was made up of the county judge and two justices of the peace. This body functioned as the Board of Supervisors until 1855, when the legislature passed an act creating the San Joaquin County Board of Supervisors, with three members, to assume the work of the Court of Sessions.

This county government was without precedent or experienced personnel, and was unable to cope with the problems of crime, streets, health and transportation in

City of Stockton
County of San Joaquin
State of California
United States of America

that turbulent time in Stockton's history. It was soon apparent that a city government was necessary. Again it was Alcalde George Belt who called a meeting in his tent store, on March 15, 1850, to organize a city government. Several other meetings were necessary to draw up incorporation provisions and to petition the Court of Sessions of San Joaquin County for an order of incorporation for the town of Stockton. On July 25, 1850 the petition was presented and was granted by Judge Benjamin Williams. The city had a population of just over two thousand. It was to be governed by a council of seven. The boundaries were to be Flora Street on the north, Aurora Street on the east, Twiggs (Anderson) Street on the south and Bragg and Tule (Edison) Streets to the west.

A slate of candidates for city officials was nominated and an election was held on August 1, 1850, in the tent of the Central Exchange. Samuel Purdy was chosen as mayor and on August 5 the first meeting of the City Council was held in the Masonic Hall. Soon the McNish Building was leased for $300 a month as a meeting place. In fact, this building was used by both county and city government and served as a courthouse and jail. It was located on the northwest corner of Hunter and Channel Streets and was a large two-story wooden building. The jail was placed in the basement. The first courthouse was not considered adequate and the courtroom was moved to the old Giraffe Hotel on Main Street west of Center.

The need for a courthouse and city hall soon became obvious, and in 1853 committees were appointed to plan for the construction of a courthouse and jail. Although the county had been levying a property tax for the building of the courthouse, the collected funds were inadequate. It was agreed that scrip or bonds bearing a ten percent interest rate should be sold to raise funds. Captain Charles Weber donated a square block bounded by San Joaquin, Main and Hunter Streets, and Weber Avenue. The location was between two sloughs, but Weber insisted on a plaza because every California town had one. It was obtained by filling in the slough on the west side, and is now Hunter Square.

The first courthouse built on this site, in 1853, was a two-story Roman Doric building and cost $84,000. Not only was it used by both the city and county but was a general community hall. Even fairs were held here until the Agricultural Hall was built on San Joaquin Street. It was dedicated on April 17, 1854, and on the same day county and city offices were occupied. Later a domed belfry with a 1900-pound bell and a large clock was added.

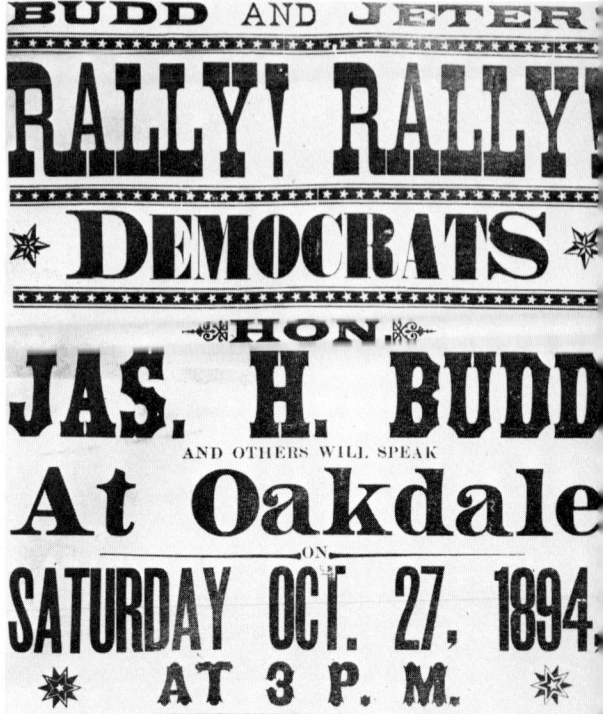

There were two cannons on the courthouse grounds, one on the northwest corner and the other on the southeast corner. They were taken from a ship once commanded by Commodore Robert Field Stockton and given to the city in 1906. Decades later they were removed and their fate is unknown.

However, by the 1870s and 1880s the deterioration of the old building and overcrowding brought recognition of the need for a new courthouse. In 1887 the building was demolished and work was begun on a larger three-story granite one on the same site. This building of Neoclassic style cost $260,000. It was completed on December 3, 1890 and soon had the reputation of being the most handsome courthouse in the state.

Until 1910 both city and county governments used the building, but with the completion of the Hotel Stockton, city offices were moved into new quarters there.

As the county grew and county government expanded, this new courthouse became inadequate and county offices were housed in various places around Stockton. The old building was showing the strain of deterioration and plans were made for a new one. Even though "authorities" claimed the old building was unsound, the voters turned down two bond issues for a new courthouse. It was not until 1960 that bonds were approved for replacing the old building on the same site. All offices were moved to the Hotel Stockton, the grand old courthouse was removed, with difficulty, and a new steel, glass and marble courthouse, costing $5,500,000, was built in its place. In 1964 a ribbon-cutting ceremony was held by the Board of Supervisors, and the new courthouse was occupied.

As Stockton has been accessible to political campaigning, with two and then three transcontinental railroads, politicians have stopped here for at least a whistle-stop talk, a few words from the rear platform on the train. Stockton has always been an active and interested political town and crowds have always shown up to hear the candidates make their promises. Both William McKinley and William Jennings Bryan campaigned here in 1896 and in their rematch in 1900. A memorial service was held for McKinley at the Agricultural Pavilion when he was killed in 1901. Bryan delivered his matchless oratory at several rallying points in the business area and paraded with the mayor in his carriage.

Charles Evans Hughes paused for a whistle-stop talk at the Southern Pacific depot in 1916. He lost California to President Woodrow Wilson and lost the election.

Even though delegates from Stockton failed in their invitation to the state legislature to move the state capital from Benicia to Stockton in 1854 and use the new courthouse as a capitol, Stockton did elect one of its illustrious lawyers to the governorship. James H. Budd, a Democrat and popular lawyer and politician, was sent to Sacramento as governor in 1895 for one term. His health failed and he did not run for a second term.

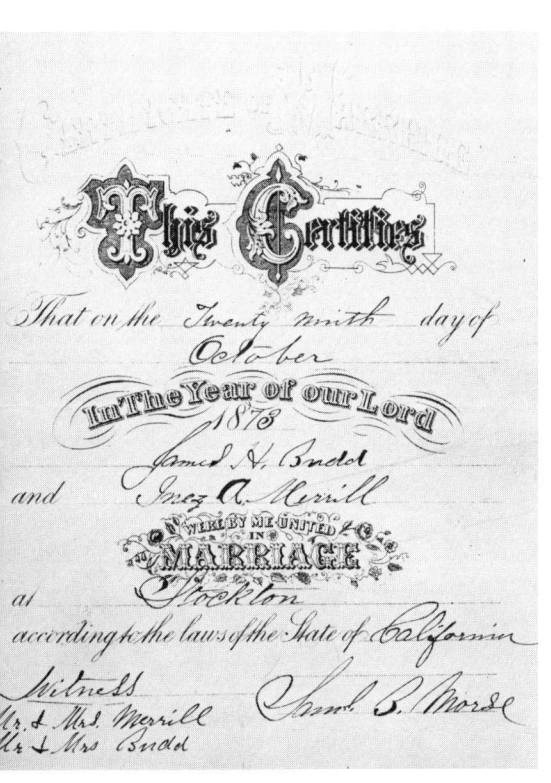

James A. Budd, California's only governor from Stockton, married Inez A. Merrill in Stockton October 29, 1873. Shown is the original marriage certificate, which is on display at the Pioneer Museum and Haggin Galleries, along with Mr. Budd's walking stick and other personal belongings.

Richard Nixon came to Stockton for a rally in Hunter Square, the most popular location for rallies, during his campaign for governor in 1962.

Both the Centennial and Bicentennial celebrations of National Independence were observed in Stockton with enormous parades and other events, all attended by large crowds. Photographs of the large parade in 1876 through the business section give us a good idea of what Stockton was like then. The Bicentennial in 1976 was observed with a two-hour-long parade, but several other events attracted larger crowds. When the Freedom Train arrived on West Weber Avenue and remained for several days, over 30,000 visitors, mostly school children, passed through the museum cars to see some of the significant American documents and objects. A giant steam locomotive that had been reconditioned in Portland, Oregon pulled the Freedom Train around the country.

Another bicentennial event that attracted national publicity was the unique unveiling, by the use of a balloon, of three bicentennial plaques, which had been placed on a 55-ton Sierra granite boulder. In 1876 an effort to hold a balloon ascension in Hunter Square was a failure. To commemorate that effort, a balloon was successfully launched in 1976 and the plaques, dedicated to Captain Charles Weber, were dramatically unveiled.

The citizens of Stockton always supported war efforts when the nation became involved. This was especially true in World War II, when Stockton became a center for storage and shipping of war materials. A Naval Annex was located at Rough and Ready Island, on the Deep Water Channel to San Francisco Bay.

Shipbuilding was a major effort in Stockton during World War II, with several construction companies turning out ships of various types on government contracts. Thousands of people were employed in this critical industry, which was concentrated largely along the north bank of the Stockton Channel.

As a concluding feature of the 1876 celebration there was to be a balloon ascension by Professor Starweather in the Hunter Square Plaza. The balloon rose to about ten feet and then fell back into the crowd. Professor Starweather let the balloon go a second time, by itself. It rose and drifted to an area near Linden, where it fell into a field.

This 1976 balloon ascension on Weber Point unveiled the monument with the plaques to Captain Charles Weber. This unique unveiling method was an imitation of the balloon ascension of 1876 and was a spectacular success. The project, which involved bringing a fifty-five-ton granite boulder down from Tuolumne County in the Sierras to be used as a monument for the three plaques, was planned and carried out by the Stockton Cultural Heritage Board with financial support from the City Council. The event received national publicity as the most unusual unveiling in history. (Photograph by Mike Cassidy)

San Joaquin County's first courthouse was built in Stockton in 1853 at a cost of $84,000. The structure was used by both the county and city and the cost was divided. This photo was taken during the flood of 1862. Notice the absence of the clocks in the dome. The Odd Fellows Lodge laid the cornerstone in this first building.

The second county courthouse was on the same location as the first. It was started in 1887, with the Masonic Lodge laying the cornerstone, and was completed in 1890. It was made of California granite and cost $260,000. This picture, taken in the 1920s, shows a panoramic view of the courthouse and Hunter Square Plaza. The courthouse remained in this location until it was torn down in 1961 to make way for our third courthouse.

After the demolition of the old courthouse, ground was broken for the construction of the new $5½ million Courts and Administration Building on November 15, 1961. On June 1, 1964, thirty-one and one-half months later, the first departments began moving into the new seven-story building from their temporary quarters. The official dedication and ribbon-cutting by the Board of Supervisors was held in 1964.

All that remained of the stately old courthouse at one point during demolition. Most of the demolition was done by hand, and hundreds of antiques were removed from the building, which had marble panels, mahogany hand rails, and Belgian tiles. Most of the courtrooms had fireplaces, solid brass door knobs, and dozens of other valuable articles. Many of these antiques are in Stockton homes as souvenirs.

Early one morning in 1961 the dome was made ready to come down. Steel cables were tied around the lower part of the dome and with two Caterpillar tractors pulling, it was soon all over—a sad sight for old-timers, and the end of an era.

James Budd was born May 18, 1851 and moved to Stockton in 1860. He attended local schools and the University of California, where he studied law. He lived in the famous Budd House on North Sutter Street with his mother and father, the Honorable Joseph Budd. He became a lawyer in 1874 and California's nineteenth governor in 1895, the only governor from Stockton.

This photograph was taken at the Inaugural Ball for Governor Budd on July 11, 1895. He is standing behind his "first lady" in the center of the group.

The James H. Budd residence on the northwest corner of Channel and Ophir Streets (Airport Way) was referred to as the Governor's Mansion. Mr. Budd served for one term, but did not run for reelection due to poor health. He died in his home on July 30, 1908.

William Jennings Bryan was in Stockton in 1896 while campaigning for the presidency. He is seated in the buggy and wearing the white hat. Seated across from him is Governor James Budd of Stockton.

A large crowd gathered at Main and El Dorado Streets to hear William Jennings Bryan speak. These were the days before microphones and a man's voice, even Mr. Bryan's strong, resonant one, would carry only so far. He made fifteen-minute speeches in several different locations around the town.

Here Mr. Bryan is speaking in the Hunter Square Plaza. He could always gather a large crowd because of his reputation as an orator.

President McKinley was here on May 26, 1901. Above, he made a twenty-minute speech from the rear platform of the train at the Southern Pacific depot. Several thousand people were there to hear him. McKinley cut his speech short as he was hurrying to the side of Mrs. McKinley, who was severely ill in San Francisco. President William McKinley was assassinated just six months after visiting Stockton. Right, at a memorial service held in the Pavilion there was standing room only.

Charles Evans Hughes, who was running for president in 1916, included Stockton among his stops. He arrived at the Southern Pacific depot on August 22 at 4:30 P.M. In this picture, taken at that time, are Hughes and his wife in the center, Stockton attorney Arthur Levinsky to the extreme left, and Francis F. Keeling and William H. Crocker to the right. Hughes looked tired and spoke to the crowd for only a few minutes. He was having voice trouble and his personal physician was with him through his entire cross country campaign.

Mr. Richard Nixon was in Stockton campaigning for Governor of California against Pat Brown in 1956. Here he is shown at Stockton Field. Left to right are Cliff Bull, Congressman Leroy Johnson, Nixon, and Senator Thomas Kuchel.

Marching along Cemetery Lane, the Spanish American War Veterans had just finished the memorial services in Rural Cemetery, early this century.

In 1946 two B29 Army planes crashed head-on over Stockton in heavy fog. One of the planes crashed into the Rindge tract about ten miles northwest of Stockton, and the other crashed into MacDonald Island about two miles from the first plane. Due to the roadways of the Delta it was nearly a thirty-minute trip from one of the planes to the other. Shown above is the removal of bodies from the plane on Rindge tract. A large amount of foamite was poured over the planes the following morning for fear the peat dirt would ignite and burn the entire island. Three airmen survived the crash, but eighteen young soldiers were killed.

Kyle and Company, located on the Stockton Channel, is shown, right, with landing craft and barges they built. Thousands of local people worked in Stockton's shipyards and defense plants during World War II. After the war the only shipbuilding yards that remained were Stephens Marine and Colberg Boat Works. Stephens Marine now builds some of the finest cruisers in the world. Colberg builds many of the sightseeing and cruise boats in the San Francisco Bay.

Top: A view along the Stockton Channel showing Stephens Brothers Shipyards in the foreground, with Colberg Boat Works just beyond. The minesweepers ready for delivery were built by Stephens in 1954 for the Korean War. Most of the shipyards were on the north bank of the Stockton Channel, including Kyle and Company, Pollack, Clyde Wood, Stephens Bros., Moore Equipment, Stockton Steel Fabricators, and Colberg Boat Works. Colberg's was started in 1896 and most of the ferries operated in the county were built here. The company's first government contract to build six minesweepers was a joint venture with Stephens, which was founded in 1902.

Air view of Pollock Shipyards in the 1940s. Some of the warships being built can be seen in the Stockton Channel.

Stockton Naval Supply Depot is located on Rough and Ready Island on the Stockton Deep Water Channel. This picture from the 1960s shows the moth-balled ships of the Pacific Reserve Fleet. One of the outstanding features of this naval base is its continuous concrete wharf 6,500 feet long, one of the largest in the world.

The 1876 Centennial Parade along Weber Avenue. On the morning of the Fourth of July at 9:00 A.M. one cannon was fired as the signal for all divisions to move to their designated starting points. Grand Marshal J. D. Peters took the sash, his badge of office, and after a brief speech of thanks he mounted his horse and gave the command to march. More than twenty-five divisions took part in the parade. There were several marching bands, including one from Oakland. However, top honors went to Stockton's own Emmett Guard Band.

Former City Manager Walter Hogan with his secretary, Miss Laura Berry. Hogan Reservoir near Valley Springs was named for him. As City Manager he was influential in getting the first dam built on the Calaveras River.

The Grand Triumphal Arch. The bases were twenty feet tall and painted red, white and blue, and there was a short tower on each side topped with golden eagles. At least a dozen flags were attached to the top. On the face of the arch was the motto "1776 E Pluribus Unum 1876." The arch was built and given to the city by Grand Marshal J. D. Peters.

This sketch by Ethelyn Wood shows John Brown delivering the message of the Los Angeles Revolt to Commodore Stockton. In 1846, during the conquest of California by the American forces under the command of Commodore Robert Stockton as military governor, a revolt occurred in the Los Angeles area and the small American detachment was surrounded and besieged by the Mexicans. Captain Gillespie, in charge, asked for a volunteer to break through the lines and take word of the revolt to Commodore Stockton, who had returned to San Francisco Bay with his fleet. John Brown, called Juan Flaco by the Americans, agreed to carry the message, and in four and one-half days, after wearing out many horses, he delivered the message to Commodore Stockton. In later years John Brown came to Stockton where he died in 1858. He lies buried somewhere on Union Street in the old cemetery. A bronze plaque was erected to this hero in 1969 at the corner of Union Street and Weber Avenue.

7 Law Enforcement

When a new country is being settled and no government has been organized, the protection of life and property is a matter for the individual. The gold rush in California attracted many criminals from all over the world. Life was hazardous and property rights were defended with guns or, in cases of extreme aggravation, by vigilante justice. Even after California became a state and local government was organized, without experienced personnel to operate the new offices, authorities were not effective in stopping rampant crime.

San Joaquin County government was organized in an election on April 1, 1850 in which county officials were chosen. The first elected sheriff, Dr. R. Porter Ashe, was sworn in on April 3. Stockton city officials were elected in August; William H. Willoughby was chosen as city marshal and sworn into office immediately. These two men were the first official law enforcement officers in the county. They must have been men of courage. The problem of maintaining order in this turbulent and restless society was tremendous. (It was claimed by one early writer that Stockton had 102 saloons at that time.)

In 1851 the San Francisco Vigilance Committee was organized by citizens to punish and drive out thieves and bandits. Many of those law-breakers fled to the gold camps of the interior and continued to prey upon law-abiding people, creating a situation that was intolerable. A vigilance committee, called Citizens Police, was organized on June 9, 1851 to curb violence, robbery, and horse thievery. Not only did the committee attempt to punish and drive the felons out of Stockton, but a committee of three met every riverboat from San Francisco. They questioned the passengers and did not permit suspicious persons to land.

The municipal council was petitioned to grant authority to the Citizens Police, but refused. Nonetheless the committeemen did manage to establish security in the districts to which they assigned themselves.

Protecting the good life in a growing community

A beloved and respected law man was Sheriff Thomas Cunningham, who served from 1871 to 1899. He was originally a saddle and harness maker and was also a Stockton fireman. The first Delta College center was named in his honor.

San Joaquin County sheriffs since Cunningham have been: Walter F. Sibley, 1899-1911; William H. Riecks, 1911-1930; Martin Ansbro, 1930-1946; Carlos A. Sousa, 1946-1960; Michael N. Canlis, 1960-1977; and Frank Harty, present sheriff.

Carlos Sousa was a popular sheriff of San Joaquin County from 1946 until his death in 1960.

Michael N. Canlis was one of San Joaquin County's outstanding sheriffs. Canlis joined the sheriff's staff in 1939. In 1942 he became superintendent of the County Bureau of Criminal Identification and Investigation. He was appointed under-sheriff in 1947 and was sworn in as sheriff in July 1960. He died on February 14, 1977 at the age of 59. Just five months earlier a recognition dinner party was given for Canlis with well over 1,000 paying generously to attend. The sign tells it all.

Jails, even temporary ones, were a problem. The brig *Susanne* was the first jail, and the basement of the McNish Building was used from 1851 until a grand jury condemned it in 1853. A new building was then built specifically for a jail. Since it was fairly secure, several of the Mother Lode counties sent their long-term prisoners to Stockton for incarceration. Although the Board of Supervisors eventually condemned this building, it was not until 1893, during the long term of Sheriff Tom Cunningham, that a new jail was constructed at San Joaquin and Channel Streets. This beautiful building, which was equipped to handle seventy-five prisoners, was dubbed "Cunningham's Castle" because of its unusual architectural features. Over the years it became badly overcrowded and began to deteriorate so plans were made to move to new facilities. In 1958 a new jail was built at French Camp, and a few years later the old jail was demolished.

San Joaquin County has had many good sheriffs; the three best-remembered are Thomas Cunningham, Carlos Sousa, and "Mike" Canlis.

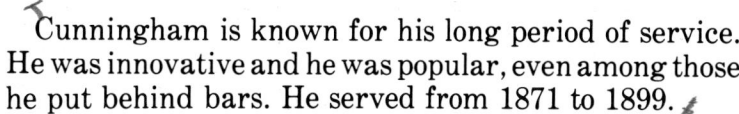

Notices posted in Chinese gambling houses gave titles, times and amounts for lottery drawings, big business in the early part of this century.

Cunningham is known for his long period of service. He was innovative and he was popular, even among those he put behind bars. He served from 1871 to 1899.

Carlos Sousa, who had been an outstanding local athlete, was also well liked. His special interest was in the prevention of delinquency through youth clubs with interesting programs. He was sheriff from 1946 to 1960.

"Mike" Canlis, whose term was from 1960 to 1977, had served with Carlos Sousa as undersheriff and became sheriff after Sousa's death. He was nationally famous for his innovations in law enforcement and for his reforms in the treatment of prisoners. For several years he was president of the National Sheriffs Association and commuted to Washington, D.C. for meetings. He was also an adviser to the Attorney General's office. A few months before his untimely death in 1977 a tremendous testimonial dinner was given for him in the Civic Auditorium by his friends.

It was not until 1898 that Stockton police officers wore uniforms. Before then they dressed in ordinary clothes but wore a large star of authority and a derby dicer. A paddy wagon was first used to take prisoners to jail in 1900.

Police facilities were in various places around town, but the department had no building of its own until recently. For years it was on Bridge Street behind the Hotel Stockton. When the new City Hall was completed in 1926, police headquarters were in the basement. As part of the West End Redevelopment program, plans were made for a new building devoted exclusively to police facilities; it was completed and occupied in 1970.

The Stockton Police Department has a fine record of law enforcement. There have been many outstanding chiefs; one of the most popular was Chief Jack O'Keefe, who not only ran an efficient organization, but participated in and encouraged preventive activities such as sports programs and clubs to keep young people involved in worthwhile pursuits.

The first building in Stockton erected expressly for a county jail was located on the north side of Market Street between San Joaquin and Hunter. It was built in 1853. Eight legal executions took place in the rear courtyard of the building. Black Bart, legendary stage robber, was imprisoned here at one time.

The San Joaquin County Jail just before the building was torn down. The jail was built in 1893 on the northeast corner of Channel and San Joaquin Streets. Because of its unusual and attractive architectural features, seldom found in a jail or prison building, it was referred to as "Cunningham's Castle." Thomas Cunningham was sheriff at the time and had a hand in its design.

This is an aerial view of the San Joaquin County Honor Farm and Jail. It is located on Mathews Road in French Camp, about five miles south of Stockton. These facilities were built in 1958.

Here are the law officers who participated in the capture of the bandit Black Bart. Notice the hatchet held by Sheriff Ben Thorn; it had been used by Bart to break open a strongbox. In the front row from left to right are: Tom Cunningham, Sheriff of San Joaquin County; Ben Thorn, Sheriff of Calaveras County; Harry Morris, detective for Wells Fargo and Co. Express. Top row: Captain Stone, Central Pacific Railroad detective, and John Thacker, detective for Wells Fargo and Co.

The demolition of the old but architecturally beautiful County Jail in 1960. Though attractive, it had been inadequate for many years. It had been built to confine seventy-five prisoners but was almost always badly overcrowded. In 1958, after several years of agitation for a new jail, correctional facilities were built near French Camp, and the old "Castle" was razed. Its site is Stockton Historical Landmark No. 10 and bears a plaque.

Stockton police officers, below, are ready to leave to assist in controlling the riot at Folsom Prison in 1937. However, it was brought under control before they arrived and they were not needed. From left to right are Cy Childs, Paul Quyle, Ernest Stuart, Ben McGlothen, Fred Gravtzow, Chief Wilbur Potter, Captain C. O. Smith, Elmer Smith, and Delbert Reynolds.

Stockton Police Chief Charles McGurk and his staff of fifteen men, in front of the courthouse c. 1900. Front row, left to right: Dan Klench, William Simpson, Chief McGurk (standing), Frank Briare, John Craig. Middle row, left to right: Westley Dutschke, Mat McDermott, Mike Finnell, Mike Carroll, Oscar Marshall, Joseph Gill. Back row, left to right: John Jackson, Walter Walker, Newton Rutherford.

The office of Police Chief was created from the position of town marshal in 1852. In 1884 the Department had eleven officers.

Left to right, Bottom Row: J. J. Joyce, F. H. Ingalls, Det. F. H. Fredericks, Det. J. C. Dewey, Capt. of Dets. C. O. Smith, City Manager Chas. E. Ashburner, Chief of Police C. W. Potter, Capt. of Police J. A. Norris, Det. A. D. Philo, Det. I. B. Washburn, Ident. Sergeant F. E. Eshbach, Clerk K. V. Eshbach.
Left to right, Second Row: R. C. Parker, Sgt. S. K. King, Sgt. V. J. Moit, Sgt. C. G. Fredericks, Sgt. H. A. Vogelsang, Lieut. E. W. Steele, Lieut. G. E. Cannon, Lieut. G. C. Smith, P. B. Quyle, J. H. Harbert, F. Grantzow, Bailiff A. W. Chance.
Left to right, Third Row: A. Cramer, J. P. Shoemaker, H. F. Strike, F. J. Murray, L. M. Booth, E. W. Thorpe, D. L. McIntosh, H. A. Sanders, T. J. Long, A. L. Owen, E. F. Stuart, W. A. McLachlan, B. H. McGlothen.
Left to right, Fourth Row: B. J. Cassidy, J. B. Patton, J. McNabb, T. J. Mandic, F. P. Brown, F. J. McHugh, H. C. Kram, R. E. McHugh, R. C. Vosburgh, L. N. Werle, D. W. Reynolds.
Left to right, Top Row: W. S. Darling, A. B. Saxton, Court Clerk H. H. Montgomery, Police Judge Cecil S. Johnson, Prosecuting Attorney C. E. Grant, C. T. Thornton, W. Childs.

Dec. 31, 1926.

This picture of the entire Stockton Police Department was made on the steps of the then brand new City Hall on December 31, 1926. Notice the only female was clerk K. V. Esbach. Today there are many women in the Department—clerks, secretaries, radio dispatchers, meter maids and policewomen.

Officer C. O. Smith and Chief C. W. Potter are checking over whiskey stills, bootleg liquor, narcotics, etc. Chief Potter is holding an opium pipe. The scene is at the west entrance of City Hall where the Police Department was located for nearly forty years.

The Stockton Police Main Facility on Market between Center and El Dorado Streets was dedicated in 1970. In the first decades of the twentieth century the department was housed on Bridge Street near El Dorado Street. In 1926 a new headquarters was established in the basement of the newly built city hall. The Police Department now has a staff of over 300. Julio Cecchetti is Chief. The force is assisted by a canine corps of German shepherds. Stockton Police Youth Activities encompass three major areas: sports, musical and marching units, and police cadets. Each year 3,000 Stockton youths are active in fifteen different activity units.

Retired Stockton police officers. Seated, left to right: Jim Dewey, C. O. Smith, Erv Washburn, Hugh Tye, and Frank McHugh. Standing: C. W. Potter, Joe Joyce, Grover Smith, and Cy Childs. This picture was taken when the group met for a dinner party in 1954.

Jack O'Keefe was Stockton's Police Chief from 1950 to 1970.

8 Fire Department

Fire was the great destroyer in all the early towns of California, especially mining camps, in their formative years. This was due to the building material used, such as canvas, brush, or wood, all highly inflammable. In addition, there was no plan or equipment for combating fires once they started. Historians have estimated the property loss from fires at $66,000,000 during the first three years of the California Gold Rush. These figures seem startling only if we fail to consider the type of building materials used and the nature of the structures. Many towns were completely destroyed two or three times. Stockton was no exception and suffered its first great fire on December 23, 1849. Hastily organized volunteer bucket brigades made an effort to contain the fire by passing wooden buckets of water to the fire along a line of men, and empty buckets back along another line to the channel. The fire destroyed the entire area, bounded by Weber Avenue, El Dorado, Main and Center Streets. The total loss was estimated at $500,000, which would indicate that the buildings were of the flimsiest materials. As a result of this fire, the first fire company was organized. It was called the Weber Bucket Brigade and was equipped with wooden buckets to be passed from hand to hand from barrels of water placed at intervals along the streets.

Stockton was the head of year round navigation on the San Joaquin River and so the town was rebuilt to continue its role as a supply port for the Southern Mines.

During this rebuilding more consideration was given to fireproof building materials, and as plans for a city government were made, fire and police protection was considered a necessity.

The Weber Engine Company #1 was established on June 26, 1850. It consisted of volunteers and was organized with James E. Nuttman as Chief.

As there were no funds for equipment, Captain Weber purchased a small hand-operated fire engine in San Francisco. In 1850 the City Council agreed to pay

---

Early-day fire losses were enormous—comparable disasters are unknown today.

Opposite page: San Joaquin Engine Company #3, as it appeared in 1873. Their headquarters, located at 509 East Weber Avenue, was built in 1869. Stockton's spirited volunteer fire companies has such slogans as: "We aim to conquer," "We strive to save," and "Sometimes rough, but always ready." The fire equipment shown in this view includes, from left to right, the pioneering chemical truck, a hose cart and an end brake hand pumper.

him $3,779 in installments for the pumper. It was a small affair called a "Garden Engine" and was housed in Weber's barn, on the Peninsula, until a sum of $1,400 was raised by subscriptions to construct the first firehouse to be located at Bridge Place and Hunter Street. Funds were also raised to purchase several ladders and hooks in October 1850. These were put on a hand-pulled wagon and kept on the Plaza.

This was the only equipment available to fight the big fire that swept through Stockton on May 5, 1851. The property loss included 101 buildings, valued at $1,500,000. The hand engine was badly damaged and the other meager fire equipment was entirely lost in this fire.

Chief Nuttman was sent to San Francisco by the City Council to purchase hose, which in those days was usually made of buffalo hides. He learned that they could not buy hose unless they bought an engine, too. The decision was made to spend the necessary $6,000, and the new engine was housed at Bridge Place and Hunter Street and taken over by the Weber Company. A hook and ladder company of thirty men was organized in November 1851, with a suitable building eventually erected on Market and San Joaquin Streets.

A second company of volunteers was formed in June 1853, because of a division among members of the Weber Company. They adopted the name of Eureka which means, "I have found it." The two companies became rivals, endeavoring to excel each other in efficiency and speed in arriving at a call.

In 1853 efforts were being made by the Eureka Company to obtain a pump when it was learned that one was available in San Francisco. Los Angeles had ordered this pump but could not raise the $4,500 needed. Chief Edwin Colt was sent to make the purchase. When the new engine arrived in December 1853, members of the fire department, dressed in their uniforms, took the pumper to Main and Center Streets, and with water from a cistern (a tank beneath the street), tested it thoroughly.

The next big fire, in February of 1855, started on El Dorado Street between Main Street and Weber Avenue. It soon consumed many of the "temporary" buildings constructed after the fire of 1851. Both fire companies, the Weber and the Eureka, did their best with the equipment available and kept the loss down to around $55,000. They were complimented by Fire Chief Colt for their fine work.

A mass meeting of three hundred indignant citizens was held in the city council chambers after the 1855 fire. They demanded that no wooden buildings be con-

FIRE CHIEFS OF STOCKTON (Paid Department)	
Michael McCann	1888-1891
Michael McCann	1907-1912
Israel Rolt	1891-1899
James Carroll	1899-1903
James Carroll	1905-1907
Will H. Knowles	1903-1905
M. D. Murphy	1913-1936
R. E. Thompson	1936-1946
Martin Cannon	1946-1948
Lyle Stevenson	1948-1965
Mitchell Coolures	1965-1973
Rodell K. Barth	1973-1975
James Clifton	1975

structed in the "downtown" area. As a result the first zoning ordinance was adopted, prohibiting the construction of wooden buildings within the limits of Levee (now West Weber), Hunter, one hundred feet south of Main Street, and west of Commerce Street.

The third volunteer fire fighting company, The San Joaquin Engine Co. No. 3, was organized in March 1854, with a small wooden building on Weber Avenue as its station. In 1856, the city purchased a lot at Weber Avenue and California Street and erected a brick building for this company. It contained the first alarm bell in town.

In 1858 a new invention, the steam pumper, was introduced and two were purchased for use by the San Francisco Fire Department. The Weber Company was determined to have one and raised funds in various ways, including $450 from the City Council. In 1862, they acquired one for $4,000 in Philadelphia. Stockton then became the second city in the state to have this innovative machine. Efforts to move the engine by hand were unsuccessful and soon Charles Ashley, who had two well-trained horses, was obtained to pull "Old Betsy," as Stockton's new pumper was known.

The Weber Company also purchased a four-wheeled hose carriage for $800 which was called the "Weber Hose Company" by those who managed it.

The San Joaquin Company obtained the first "Soda-Water Wagon," a chemical engine, in the state. This was in 1873. It was shown off in both Sacramento and San Francisco. It served until its replacement by a motorized truck and is still preserved in the Pioneer Museum and Haggin Galleries in Victory Park.

No objective would be achieved by listing all the fires that threatened this growing community, but the continuing threat of fire elicited new inventions and precautions. One of these was the construction of cisterns to collect rain water at all downtown intersections. At one time there were fourteen of these cisterns, which were used by the pumpers for a water supply before fire hydrants were installed in 1891.

As early as 1854, the fire companies were supervised by a board of delegates presided over by a fire chief. He served without pay until 1864 when he became the only member to receive a salary, which was $20 a month. However, the colorful period of volunteers ended on January 15, 1888, when the practice was stopped and a paid department was organized. The drivers were required to be on duty at all times. Two extra men were "on call" and came running at the first sound of the bell at the Eureka Engine House. This signal bell was replaced by a steam fire whistle at the Stockton Gas,

---

DATES IN FIRE FIGHTING

A chronolgy of historic years for the Stockton Fire Department:

1850 First hand engine.
1862 First steam engine.
1869 First time horses used.
1873 Arrival of pioneering chemical truck.
1881 Alarm boxes installed.
1888 Paid department replaces volunteers.
1891 Fire hydrants first put on corners in the business district.
1913 Mechanization of the department starts.
1924 Last horses retired. (Hook and ladder)

One of Stockton's horse drawn steamers used for pumping water by steam power from sloughs or cisterns. A fire was lighted in the boiler as soon as the engine left the fire house and when it arrived at the fire, there would be a full head of steam.

Light and Heat Company, located at Center Street and Hazelton Avenue.

In later years, many great fires occurred in Stockton but it would be repititious to describe all of them. The Pavilion fire of September 28, 1902, however, was talked about for many years. When built, the Pavilion boasted 38,000 feet of floor space, was constructed of wood and was in the form of a cross. It cost $50,000 and occupied the block bounded by Washington, San Joaquin, Lafayette and Hunter Streets. The largest hall in Stockton, it was used for agricultural fairs, dances, concerts, political rallies, and such.

During the great fire, a fireman of the Eureka, Thomas J. Walsh, lost his life in an effort to save his horse. While fighting the fire on Lafayette Street, he made the mistake of pulling the hose cart too close to the fire. He was the first fireman lost in the fifty-two-year history of the Stockton Fire Department.

The Pavilion fire was carried by a strong north wind and traveled south to Church and San Joaquin Streets. Fifty residences and forty-five other buildings were destroyed, including the Santa Fe Hospital. As the hospital burned, a large storage tank of ether exploded, sending writhing, blue flames at least two hundred feet into the air.

Eureka Engine #2 at 25 South Hunter Street. Notice the hard rubber tires and the early gasoline powered equipment. Stockton's first motorized fire fighting equipment was bought in 1913.

Headquarters of Engine Co. #3 at Pilgrim Street, north of Main Street. Some of the latest equipment, for 1908, is being shown in front of the new, not yet occupied, fire house. This building still stands today, but is no longer a fire house.

Weber Engine Company #1, Stockton's first fire company. The building at 25 East Channel was erected in 1863. The equipment is a steam pumper (right) and a hook and ladder truck.

Sperry's Flouring Mills fire on West Weber Avenue at Madison Street, on April 2, 1882. The fire completely destroyed the mills.

The rapidly burning Pavilion building, once the largest structure in Stockton. It was completed in the late 1880s and burned to the ground the morning of September 28, 1902. The beautiful building before the fire may be seen on page 56.

This action photo was taken for publicity purposes on the second floor of the Pilgrim Street fire house c. 1910. The men would slide down a brass pole to the floor below, hitch up the horses and go. All this action took place in less than three minutes.

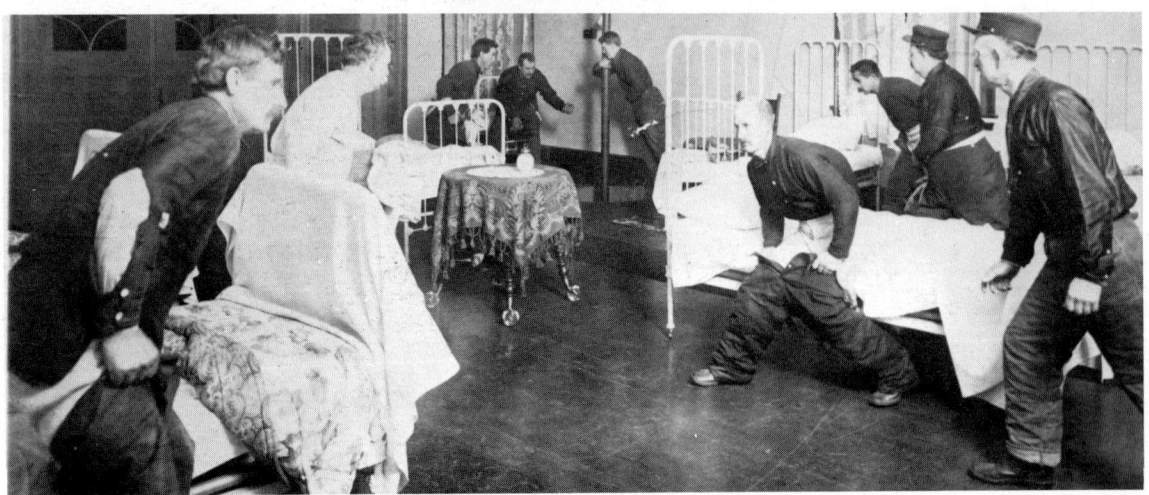

The Commercial Bank fire of 1923. The fire started in the Hotel Philson on Sutter Street and destroyed a quarter of a block at Main and Sutter Streets. The bank building was repaired by Shepherd and Green, contractors, and reopened as the main branch of the Bank of America.

Fire Chief M. D. Murphy. He first entered the fire department on June 1, 1890 as call-man. In 1905 he was made a full-pay member and was stationed at the chemical house. When M. McCann was made chief of the department, Murphy was appointed as his assistant. He was made chief upon McCann's retirement and served from 1913 to 1936.

Popular Stockton Fire Chief Ralph E. Thompson, who served from 1936 to 1946.

The Eden Square Apartments fire of 1933. The fire started early one Sunday morning and the flames could be seen for miles. The apartment house was repaired and is still in use today at El Dorado and Acacia Streets. (Photograph by Al Silva)

This view, above, along San Joaquin Street at Main Street, shows a large crowd watching firemen working at the Smith and Lang fire of the previous day, July 23, 1958. The store was rebuilt and opened as Weinstock's.

A train mishap on May 28, 1969 at Hemet Avenue just south of Hammer Lane, along the Western Pacific Railroad tracks. The box cars were derailed and caught fire. Nearby residents were worried that their houses would catch on fire.

The Central Fire Station at 110 West Sonora Street opened in December 1960. The department now has 207 men in uniform and nine substation buildings.

9 Agriculture

Stockton has been a farming community from early in its history, beginning with disappointed gold seekers who turned to farming where "gold" could be reaped more dependably. Soon San Joaquin County became an agricultural center and Stockton a shipping port for one of the great wheat growing areas in the nation. As the rich San Joaquin Delta lands were reclaimed with the encouragement of the Swamp Act of 1850, making the land available for one dollar an acre, an immensely fertile area was added to local resources.

California the "fabulous" is made up of many things—the highest mountain, the lowest valley, the highest waterfalls—but its fame comes mostly from its agriculture. For the last thirty years California has been in first place among the states in value of agricultural products, followed by the state of Iowa, according to a report from the State Department of Food and Agriculture. The gross value of California agricultural products in 1976 was $8.9 billion, including livestock. The reason for this leadership is not only the size of the state but the variety of climates which make possible specialty crops. Something is being harvested during each season of the year. It is claimed that in the United States a total of over 215 different agricultural products are grown, and almost all of these are produced in California. The reliance upon irrigation is important—one-fourth of all the irrigated land in the nation is in California. Historians estimate the value of all the gold produced in California at about $3.3 billion dollars. Comparing this amount with the total value of agriculture each year makes it obvious where the gold is produced today—on the farms.

California's agriculture is centered in the great Sacramento and San Joaquin Valleys, and Stockton is the shipping point for the latter, with its inland port, three major transcontinental railroads, and highways. Among the leading crops grown in San Joaquin County are grapes, tomatoes, almonds, cherries, corn, sugar beets, and asparagus. Milk is the leading farm product of the county.

The gold from the mines has been surpassed by the "gold" of rich farm lands.

The era of grain growing in the area continued to the 1890s and led to businesses locating in Stockton to process the crop. Austin Sperry and George Lyons established Stockton's first flour mill in 1852. At first they had to import some of the grain from outside the area, but by 1856 enough wheat of superior quality was grown locally to keep the mill in full operation. Soon they developed their famous "Drifted Snow Flour." Although other flour mills were established, most were eventually acquired by Sperry and in the 1890s the firm was the largest flour milling operation in the state. By the 1920s, more lucrative irrigated crops and competition from other areas of the country forced the Sperry mill in Stockton to close. However, still well preserved is the former Sperry Flour Mill office at Weber Avenue and Madison Street. This attractive Victorian brick office building was completed in 1888 and served the company until it closed. It was scheduled for demolition in 1968, but a group of concerned local Stocktonians organized a successful campaign to save the building. It now serves as an attorney's office.

Another effect of the wheat-growing period on businesses of Stockton was the development of the combined harvester, which was a combination of a header or reaper and a threshing machine. Such machines made it possible to cut, thresh, clean and sack grain with one machine being pulled through the field. Although several firms made standard harvesters locally, it was the Holt Manufacturing Company that built the first side-hill harvester that made possible the growing and harvesting of wheat in the rolling hill country, not only of the foothills of California, but in Oregon, Washington, and the Dakotas.

The Holt brothers, Charles and Benjamin, located in Stockton in 1883 and established the Stockton Wheel Company, specializing in hardwood lumber and wagon parts. They soon expanded their efforts to farm machinery. They were not only concerned with the side-hill harvester, but with harvesting grain in the soft peat soil of the Delta where extensions to the wheels of the harvester resulted in extending them thirty-six feet from one side of the machine to the other. They were unwieldy and cumbersome. It was Benjamin Holt and his associates who met this need by inventing and perfecting the Caterpillar track-type tractor. The idea was to design a tractor that could pick up and lay down its own footing in the soft peat soil. In 1906 the first commercial model crawler was sold; this steam rig encouraged further developments. By 1908 the tractors were driven by gasoline engines. During World War I large orders

> The ten leading agricultural products in San Joaquin County in 1976 were (in descending order): milk, grapes, hay, tomatoes, eggs, almonds, cherries, corn, sugar beets, and asparagus. Together they had a gross value of $342,963,490.

> 843,876,000 eggs were produced by San Joaquin County chickens in 1976.

> 315,000 acres of San Joaquin County were in pasture and range in 1976. 52,161 acres were devoted to grapes, and 31,030 to tomatoes.

Figures from San Joaquin County Agricultural Report - 1976
Published by San Joaquin County Department of Agriculture

for this type tractor came from the American, British, French, and Russian governments. The tractors were used to haul artillery and supplies.

The British developed the possibility of adapting the Holt track laying principle to a moving fortress called a tank. These British tanks were successful in the closing months of World War I. In 1925 Holt merged with the Best Tractor Company of San Leandro, California, and became the Caterpillar Tractor Company. Tractor assembly was transferred to San Leandro and to Peoria, Illinois.

Other harvester manufacturers were Harris, Matteson and Williamson, Shippe and Houser-Haines, and there were several other businesses whose existence was based on agriculture.

The LeTourneau scraper, a well known land leveling device, was invented in Stockton by Robert LeTourneau in 1919. The H. C. Shaw Plow Company can trace its origin to gold rush days.

The reclamation of Delta swamplands had its effect on Stockton business, too. The Stockton Iron Works, tracing its origin to 1868, produced equipment used in reclaiming the Delta. Their best known invention was the California Type Stockton Clamshell Bucket for constructing levees and dredging channels. It is claimed that the side-draft dredges, using these buckets, were responsible for building most of the levees in the San Joaquin Delta. Later the Stockton Iron Works developed a land dredger mounted on Holt Caterpillar tracks for digging canals across the land.

As these rich San Joaquin River Delta islands, made up of decayed plant material called peat, were reclaimed, they were devoted to crops producing abundant harvests, such as asparagus, corn, grain, onions, and potatoes.

Two names are connected with the business of agriculture in this area: Luther Burbank and George Shima. Burbank was a great scientist and biologist who developed some forty-six new plant species, and Shima was a Delta farmer who became known as the "Potato King" of the Delta.

Burbank had experimented for years with improving the quality of the potato and the species he developed is known as the Burbank potato. During the potato-growing era, from the 1890s through the 1920s, Stockton held an annual Potato Day, which was really a mini-fair. In 1923 Burbank was a special guest of the City at the Potato Day celebration, riding with Mayor Oullahan in the parade and test driving one of the Holt track-type tractors on George Shima's ranch at Woodward Island.

George Shima became interested in growing potatoes

Stockton was once called the "City of Windmills." Windmills were not only used by farmers but also within the city for domestic water systems at private homes. The first ones in Stockton were made in 1858 by the John S. Davis Company, located on Commerce between Main and Levee (now Weber) Streets. One year that company produced sixty windmills.

Other windmill manufacturers were Geddings and Hartwell, located on the northeast corner of Main and San Joaquin Streets, and Relief Windmill Manufacturers owned by A. M. Abbott, at Main and California Streets.

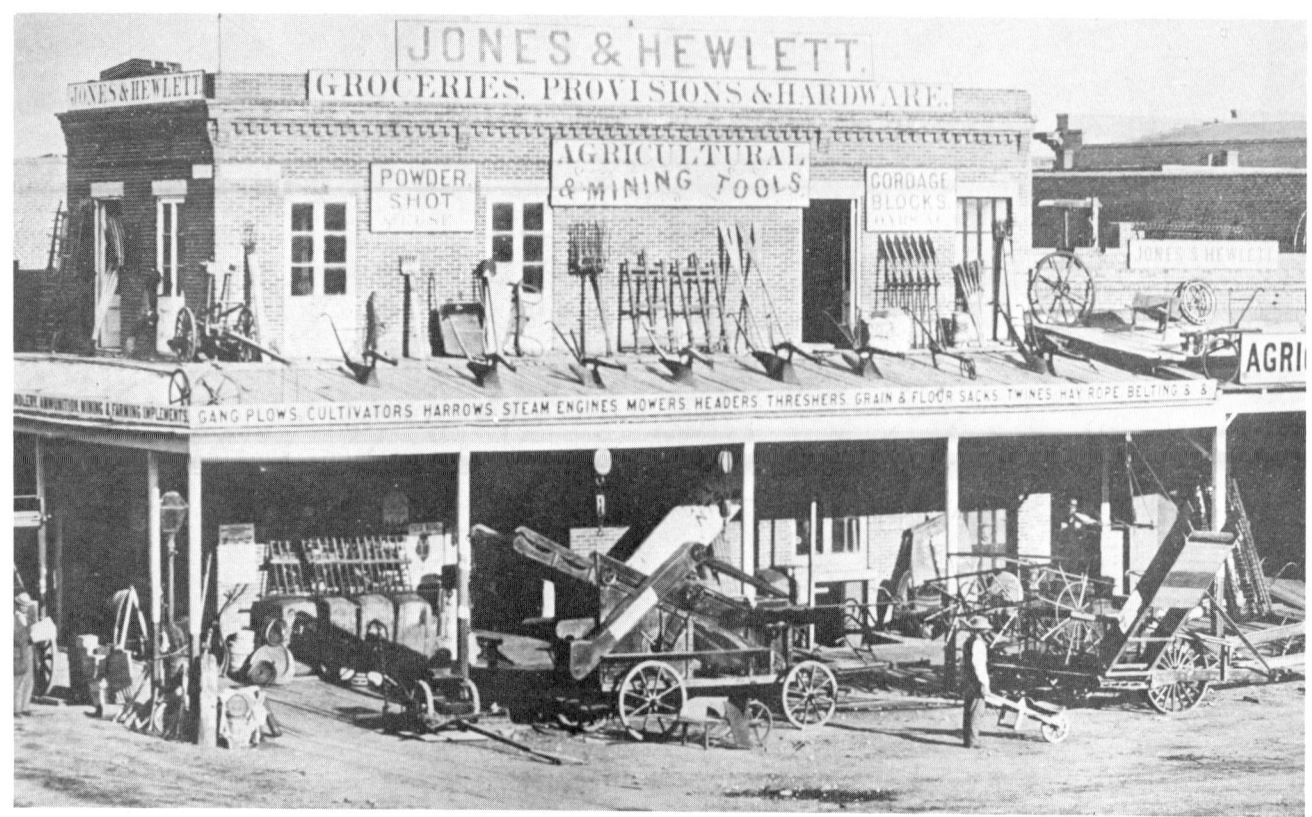

as early as 1889 when he planted his first crop on rented land near the Mokelumne River. With the profits of each year he would rent larger acreage, always making the best use of his land by successfully crossing varieties to obtain species suited to the Delta soil. By this method he was able to produce as many as 150 sacks per acre, a yield of one-third more than that obtained by adjoining farmers. He was just as successful in producing abundant harvests of onions. In 1920 he was described as the biggest food producer in the world. He owned 4,000 acres of Delta land and rented another 14,000 acres, producing potatoes, onions, asparagus, and other foods. He successfully reclaimed Delta swampland; the Shima tract north of Stockton is the best known.

Stockton was his address starting in 1892 and continuing even after his residence was established in Berkeley and San Francisco. His success greatly affected Stockton and San Joaquin County for a period of about forty years, until his death in 1926. His interest in and support of education, especially among ambitious and deserving "Nisei," made it appropriate for the San Joaquin Delta College to name one of its five new centers after him.

In its 127-year-old history, the continuing and constant influence that has shaped Stockton's growth has been the San Joaquin Delta and the rich agricultural region around it.

Jones and Hewlett at Main and Hunter Streets, established in 1851, were importers and dealers in farm implements. They sold the celebrated chisel cultivators, hand- and horse-powered seed sowers, fanning mills, hay and straw cutters, corn shellers, road scrapers, etc.

Steam threshing outfit on the John C. Kerr Ranch, located west of Lockeford. San Joaquin County in the 1880s was one of the leading grain farming areas in the nation. Wheat is still an important crop. In 1976, 41,577 acres were devoted to growing wheat with a total value of $13,637,000.

Left, a representative of the dairy business in San Joaquin County. Milk is the number one farm product in the county, with a gross value of $72,917,000 in 1976. This ribbon-winning Holstein is shown with her owner, Arthur Stoyt of Escalon, one of the county's many independent dairymen.

Below, the Ospital ranch, seven miles east of Bellota on Ospital Road. Supplemental feeding of livestock was a common sight in the range land of San Joaquin County during 1976 and 1977. Drought conditions forced the livestock industry to feed increased amounts of hay in order to maintain herds.

There are 27,000 acres devoted to asparagus in the San Joaquin Delta. This picture taken on Victoria Island in about 1935 shows workers cutting asparagus. Filipino emigrants have contributed a great deal to the agricultural development of this area.

This photograph, taken in 1958, shows the methods still employed today in the asparagus beds. The crop is gathered in powered sleds and taken to packing houses nearby. Harvesting begins in March and is usually completed around July 4. The Sacramento-San Joaquin Delta raises about seventy percent of the asparagus grown in the state.

Freshly picked asparagus is brought to the packing sheds, washed, cut, and carefully graded. Some is sent to canneries and frozen food plants; still more is packed in wet moss for shipment to distant wholesale markets. This is Morris Crudeli's packing shed on Bacon Island, 1958.

A tomato field being harvested by hand during the 1950s, near French Camp. The white dots are the hats of tomato pickers.

There has been very little hand picking of canning tomatoes since the tomato harvester was developed, but in 1958, when this picture was taken, it was a common sight.

A tomato harvester. Since 1970 a special type of tomato has been planted for mechanized harvesting. There are about 34,000 acres of tomatoes, averaging twenty-three tons per acre, in San Joaquin County. In 1977 tomatoes were in fourth place among the leading crops in the county.

Shaking walnut trees with long bamboo poles was a back-breaking job. It took many man hours to gather a few sacks of walnuts. This picture was taken in about 1915. Today harvesting of walnuts is a much different process, as shown above right in picture taken on the Anderson ranch near Linden. The walnuts are shaken from the tree by a motorized device which has a long arm with claws that clamp around the tree trunk. A few shakes bring most of the nuts to the ground. The next step is a sweep machine that rakes the nuts into wind rows. Finally the pickup machine sucks up the walnuts like a vacuum cleaner, blowing the dirt and leaves to one side while the nuts are conveyed to a trailer. With these pieces of machinery three men can handle about twenty-five acres a day or about thirty-five tons of walnuts.

San Joaquin County is in third place among California counties in walnut production, with 26,400 acres of walnut orchards.

1977 air view of Diamond Walnut Growers, Inc. (now Diamond Sunsweet), just north of the East Charter Way and Mariposa Road intersection. One of the largest processors of walnuts in the nation, this company has its headquarters in Stockton. There are thirteen acres under one roof with a railroad spur track through part of the building. Ninety-five percent of the nation's walnuts are grown in California and processed through the Stockton plant.

The Walnut Association started in Los Angeles in 1912 and moved to Stockton in 1956.

To dramatize rich San Joaquin County farm lands, infrared film was used to create the contrast in this photograph. This crop of young sugar beets is in the upper Jones tract. Sugar beets are one of the county's ten leading crops with over 36,000 acres grown in 1976.

A Southern Pacific fruit train heading north. This view is just west of Micke Grove, near Lodi. The famous Tokay grapes can be seen in the foreground. Of San Joaquin County's ten leading crops in 1976, grapes were in second place with 52,161 acres producing a $44,484,500 crop.

These two photographs illustrate how the first Holt track-type tractor was built. The experimental machine was a modification of one that had been built by Holt Manufacturing Co. for about ten years. The round wheels were removed and replaced by a platform wheel with wooden cleats. The machine was successfully tested in 1904 and was the beginning of the immense success of the company in developing and marketing what is known today as a Caterpillar track-type tractor.

On October 10, 1895, as a publicity stunt to illustrate the simplicity of operation of a Holt Brothers combined harvester, these four young ladies showed up at the Lamburth Ranch where a harvester was at work and demanded the surrender of the machine from the men in charge. The men retired from their positions and the young ladies assumed full control. Miss Ora Dowell guided the twenty-six head of horses around the field; Miss Gertie Sawyer attended the header; Miss Lillie Dowell was sack-sewer; and Miss Nellie Packwood attended to the separator. The young ladies remained in full charge for nearly four hours, then retired and turned the harvester back to the men.

An early gasoline-driven track-type tractor undergoing tests in Stockton in 1908. The gentleman who took the picture was company photographer Charles Clements. He made the remark, "My, it crawls like a caterpillar;" hence the famous name Caterpillar.

An unusual sight are these five Holt side-hill combines pulled by 165 mules and horses. This scene, taken near Walla Walla, Washington in 1904, was not only extensively used by the company for publicity but also appeared for years in geography books.

By World War I, when this photograph was taken, the plant of the Holt Manufacturing Company occupied six square blocks around South Aurora and Church Streets and employed 3,000 men. During this time the company developed not only a national market, but a world market and a large export business. Tractor manufacturing was moved to San Leandro in 1925, leaving only the combined harvester assembly lines, which were discontinued in 1929. The world headquarters of the Caterpillar Tractor Company is now in Peoria, Illinois.

This scene shows a gathering of Holt employees in front of the office building at Aurora and Church Streets in 1918. The occasion was a visit by Major General Ernest Swinton, a leading figure in the development of the British tank. Swinton and Benjamin Holt are standing beside a wooden mock-up of the tank whose success was made possible by the adaptation of the Caterpillar wheels.

The Holt Brothers' annual parade, about 1920, along Weber Avenue, with a "Caterpillar 18" in the lead. For a number of years the company proudly displayed its latest farm equipment in a parade, after which employees and their families spent the rest of the day at a picnic in Oak Park.

George Shima was born in Japan. From 1872 until his death in 1926, he lived in Stockton and farmed in the Delta. Starting with nothing, he built a highly successful farming operation of 18,000 acres and became known as the "potato king." He was an able linguist, speaking the English language fluently. A leader among his people, he believed in education and sponsored many student scholarships. A Delta College center was named in his honor.

During Luther Burbank's visit to Stockton in 1923, he toured the George Shima Ranch on Woodward Island and tried a new Holt "5 Ton" in the potato field. Another picture taken at the time of Burbank's visit is on page 152.

Stockton gang plow on the Shima Ranch, Woodward Island, in 1912. This implement was developed for use on huge acreages and made it possible to open as many as seven furrows at one time. The plow shown here is a "four bottom" that could open four furrows at a time.

All of Shima's ranch houses were built in this style. This one, shown in about 1911, was on Bacon Island. Notice the pagoda-type gate and the "high water basement."

10 Education

*A lasting legacy for all—
unlimited opportunities
for learning*

In spite of the fact that in its earliest years Stockton was influenced mainly by men on their way to the gold mines, there was interest in schools and education almost from the beginning. In the early 1850s, as permanent buildings and residences were erected, concern was expressed about educating the children of the settlement.

In 1852 an ordinance was passed providing for a Board of Education and a City Superintendent of Schools to be appointed by the City Council. They were to plan a system of free education for all the children of Stockton. Valentine Mason Peyton became president of the School Board and Dr. E. B. Bateman was appointed as the first superintendent.

In March 1853 the first public schools opened in Stockton. They were segregated, with the sixty-seven girls being taught in quarters on the north side of Main Street at a location now occupied by the Union Safe Bank. Eighty-eight boys received instruction in a building just a block away at Market and San Joaquin Streets.

Those classrooms were crowded and unsatisfactory, as were succeeding ones—moves were made with some frequency—but it was several years before the first building expressly constructed as a public school was erected. Franklin School, a two-story structure, was built at Center and Washington Streets on land donated by Captain Weber. It was torn down in 1959, 100 years after it was first occupied.

Other early school buildings were Lafayette School at San Joaquin and Market Streets, built in 1864, and Washington School at San Joaquin and Lindsay. The first high school classes, with 28 students, were taught in the front rooms of the Washington School in 1870, with A. H. Randall as principal. Washington was used for high school classes until 1904, when the Stockton High School was completed on a campus at California and Vine Streets.

All but one of these early school buildings have been removed because they did not meet code requirements against earthquake damage set up by the state legislature. The lone survivor is the old Weber school building which was erected in 1873 at a cost of $12,000 at 55 West Flora Street. It has been declared a Stockton Historical Landmark as it is the earliest brick building in Stockton retaining its original appearance; it is also on the National Register of Historic Places as it is a rare example of early public building architecture.

By 1862 there were 787 students and the Board found it necessary to establish coeducation even though there were some protests.

The first schools represented a wide mixture of nationalities, but black and Indian children were not permitted to attend. The black residents organized their own school in 1860 and in 1867 a new building was constructed for them on land donated by Captain Weber. It was not until 1879 that black students were admitted into the public schools.

The curriculum in the first schools was limited to the fundamentals: geography, United States history, natural philosophy, arithmetic, grammar, composition, spelling and penmanship.

The most significant development in education in Stockton, especially higher education, was the decision to move the historic old College of the Pacific, chartered in 1851, from San Jose to Stockton.

Dr. Tully C. Knoles, from the History Department of the University of Southern California, was invited by the Board of Regents to become president of the College of the Pacific in 1919. He found the little independent Methodist college being slowly destroyed by competition with several institutions of higher learning in the immediate vicinity. San Jose State, University of Santa Clara, Stanford University, Mills College, and the University of California were competing for the same students. Dr. Knoles studied several possible solutions, but when he learned that Stockton was the most populous city in the state without a college or university, he persuaded the Board of Regents to approve a move there.

With the cooperation and energetic support of the Chamber of Commerce, then headed by Eugene Wilhoit, a forty-acre site for a campus was obtained as a gift from the J. C. Smith Company, and a fund of $1,250,000 was raised for construction of buildings on the site.

Freshman classes were held in the new Stockton *Record* building in 1923 and in April of the following year the first bricks were laid on the new campus.

Classes were started in yet-to-be-completed buildings in September. Beginning with an enrollment of 500, the college grew and expanded thanks to the intelligent leadership of Dr. Knoles and the less competitive environment. The raw and barren campus was gradually improved with lawns, shrubs and trees and became the beautiful campus we know today. Buildings were added, course offerings were enlarged and student enrollment gradually increased.

During the twenty-seven years that Dr. Knoles was president of the College of the Pacific, the nation went through two major crises: the Depression years of 1929 to 1933, and World War II, 1942 to 1945. During the Depression the faculty showed its loyalty by agreeing to take a reduction in salary to keep the college running. During the war the college contracted with the federal government to establish a Navy V-12 program which combined an engineering curriculum with training for an ensign's commission.

In the field of sports in this period, one event occurred that was significant—the arrival of the great football coach, Amos Alonzo Stagg, from the University of Chicago. Dr. Knoles thoroughly enjoyed and supported the school's football program, and when he learned that Stagg had reached retirement age but was still physically capable and alert, he invited him to come to Pacific as the head football coach. In 1933, when Stagg and his devoted wife, Stella, came to Pacific, Dr. Knoles and many friends met the train at Sacramento and formed a caravan back to Stockton that became a parade through the downtown. It became national news and Pacific received much favorable publicity.

Stagg had many triumphs in the fourteen years of his second career. One was in 1938 when he took his Pacific team to play the University of Chicago, and they won, 32 to 0. Another was in 1943 when his great Pacific football team, bolstered by Navy V-12 players, lost only two of nine games and Stagg was voted "Coach of the Year" by the Football Coaches Association. This success brought great satisfaction to Dr. Knoles and the community of Stockton, as well as to Stagg.

In 1946 Dr. Knoles retired after twenty-seven years as president. His assistant, Dr. Robert E. Burns, was appointed twentieth president of the college at Knoles' recommendation. Dr. Knoles became chancellor.

The years of Dr. Burns' presidency have been covered fully in a volume published by the University of the Pacific in 1977, *Pioneer or Perish* by Kara Pratt Brewer, but many innovations and much expansion occurred during those years and some of the most important

events should be mentioned here.

One of the first major changes was the building of the Pacific Memorial Stadium in 1950, with a capacity of 35,000, to replace Baxter Stadium with its 10,000-seat capacity. This was made necessary by the Stagg football era, the success of Stagg's successor, Larry Semmering, and the exploits of a dazzling little quarterback from Oakdale, Eddie LeBaron.

In 1955 the Irving Martin Library, a gift from the publisher of the Stockton *Record*, Irving Martin, Sr., was built, a long-needed addition to the campus.

The cluster college idea of expansion, "growing larger by growing smaller," was the product of the thinking and planning of Dr. Burns and Ted Baun, president of the Board of Regents. Three of these smaller colleges, Raymond (1962), Elbert Covell (1963), and Callison (1967), were organized and built during the Burns years. The cluster college buildings were constructed on the site of Baxter Stadium.

Another major addition to the campus was beautiful Burns Tower, an unusual combination of a water tank and administrative offices, built in 1963. In 1966 the Donald Wood addition to the Martin Library doubled its capacity. The Wendell Phillips Center was added in 1968, and a year later the School of Pharmacy buildings and the DeMarcus Brown Theatre were completed.

The name change in 1960 from College of Pacific to University of the Pacific is noteworthy. The institution was chartered as a university, but in the first decade of the twentieth century the name was changed to college. By the 1960s this was not adequate terminology and often caused trouble with foreign students' transcripts.

Many more events of significance occurred during the presidency of Dr. Burns. These few events and developments hardly tell the whole story. During his years as president, the University became a great and famous educational institution. Dr. Burns died on February 13, 1971 and Dr. Alistair McCrone served as interim president until a new selection could be made. Dr. Stanley E. McCaffrey was named the twenty-first president of the University on October 8, 1971.

Under the enthusiastic leadership of Dr. McCaffrey the University has continued to expand. The University College and University Without Walls were established in 1972 to enable mature students to draw from all divisions of the University to earn a bachelor's degree.

In 1974 at a cost of $4,000,000 Dr. McCaffrey completed efforts to purchase the adjoining San Joaquin Delta College campus of 42 acres and nine permanent classroom buildings, a plan that Dr. Burns had initiated as early as 1958. The Delta buildings on this south campus bounded by Kensington Way and Stadium Drive are being remodeled. The former library building is the School of Education, and the largest reading room has become the Holt-Atherton Pacific Center for Western Studies, which includes the Stuart Library of Western Americana. The Speech Arts Auditorium has been extensively remodeled as a performing arts center by a $600,000 gift from Regent Thomas Long, and has been renamed the Long Theatre.

In the six years of Dr. McCaffrey's presidency enrollment figures have increased 11.3 percent. In 1974 the largest entering class in UOP history was welcomed. More than 5,700 students are enrolled at the University in 1977, including all branches of the institution.

The annual budget has increased from $22 million in 1971-72 to more than $35 million in 1976-77, and the plant value has increased by some 50 per cent, to $60 million. Endowments have increased during this period, from $3.5 million to some $8 million in 1977.

On the occasion of the 120th commencement in May 1977, Dr. McCaffrey expressed pride in what had been achieved during his presidency and confidence that the continued improvement of facilities and increase in enrollment presented a bright and promising future for the University.

Stockton's other fine educational institution is San Joaquin Delta College, which had its beginning in 1935 on the College of the Pacific campus, when Dr. Knoles and Stockton School Superintendent Andrew R. Hill persuaded the Stockton Unified School Board to organize the Stockton Junior College on the Pacific campus. This arrangement was so unusual that special legislation had to be passed for the State to permit a public junior college to operate on a private, religious college campus. Mr. Dwayne Orton was the first principal, and administration was vested in the Stockton Unified School District. At first all classes were held in rented classroom space at Pacific with a joint faculty and lower division classes were discontinued at Pacific. For several years this was a successful arrangement, but conflicts and problems eventually arose and the two educational institutions were gradually separated.

In 1949 a 42-acre site was acquired across Stadium Drive for the Stockton Junior College campus. During the following year the name was changed to Stockton College. As enrollment grew World War II surplus buildings were acquired to supplement the permanent buildings. Pacific restored its freshman and sophomore years and the joint faculty was discontinued. The two schools were completely separated by the 1950s.

Instruction centers and other facilities have been named for outstanding citizens of Stockton and San Joaquin County, as follows:
Cunningham Center - Thomas Cunningham, sheriff; *Holt Center* - Benjamin Holt, industrialist; *Budd Center* - James Budd, Governor; *Shima Center* - George Shima, farmer; *Locke Center* - Dr. Dean Jewett Locke, pioneer; *Atherton Auditorium* - Warren Atherton, attorney; *Lewis Little Theatre* - Tillie Lewis, industrialist; *Blanchard Gymnasium* - Joseph Blanchard, educator; *Ferguson Pool* - June Ferguson, educator; *Burke Bradley Drive* - Dr. Burke Bradley, President of Delta College.

By the early 1960s increased agitation developed for a junior college district separate from Stockton Unified. Plans were made for an election to set up an independent district serving high schools throughout San Joaquin County as well as parts of Sacramento, Calaveras, Amador and Solano Counties.

Under the leadership of Dr. Burke Bradley this was achieved in an election in 1963. At that time a new name was adopted and Stockton College became the San Joaquin Delta College, an independent institution with its own seven-member Board of Trustees.

A larger campus with additional buildings and facilities seemed necessary, but a bond election failed.

With the retirement of Dr. Bradley, the Board of Trustees employed Dr. Julio Bortalazzo as president with the special charge of getting a bond issue passed to finance buildings on the new campus which had been acquired from the State Hospital at Yokuts and Pacific Avenues.

Dr. Bortalazzo proved to be an energetic campaigner and succeeded in obtaining voter approval of a bond issue of $31,000,000 in 1968.

One of the appeals to the voters was that all the latest educational and technical knowledge available was to be incorporated in the construction of the new college. The buildings would be organized around a "center" which would tend to be specialized and yet fit together in a coordinated pattern. This plan has been carried out and each of the centers has been named for an outstanding historical figure in the history of Stockton and San Joaquin County.

Dr. Bortalazzo retired soon after the bond election and the responsibility of financing and building the new college was given to the new president, Dr. Joseph Blanchard and his consultant, Dr. James Keane. Over a period of four years the move from the old campus was carried out in stages as each new center was completed. During 1977-78 the campus expects to serve 19,000 day and evening students. Today the beautiful modern, tree-shaded Delta College campus, which cost about $55 million, is probably the finest community college, not only in California, but in the nation.

The Lincoln School, established in 1878 with twenty-nine students, was located along Lower Sacramento Road (now Pacific Avenue) just south of the present Lincoln Grammar School. Eight grades were taught. The school was in use until the late 1950s.

Stockton's first high school was opened in part of this building in 1870, with twenty-eight pupils attending. In 1905 the building became the Washington Grammar School and later it became the offices of the Unified School District. Today the location is a parking lot for the Bank of Stockton.

The old Stockton High School campus in 1932, known in more recent years as Stockton Junior High School. It is bounded by Harding Way, California, Vine, and San Joaquin Streets. When the school was established there were many complaints that the site was too far from the center of town. In the center right is the domed main building, which was the first built on the site and served from 1904 to 1967. Directly behind the main building are the gymnasium and science building, which were built in 1913. The low buildings to the left of the science building were also built in 1913 and were used for manual training classes. The two large buildings on San Joaquin Street are the auditorium (1924) and the cafeteria. The 2,400-seat auditorium was used by the Stockton Symphony and other performing arts groups for many years.

The first El Dorado School (1890-1915) was located on the northwest corner of El Dorado and Vine Streets. Today the beautiful Presbyterian Church is located there.

The El Dorado School built in 1916 at Harding Way and Pacific Avenue. The building was recently declared unsafe and was to be torn down, but because of the efforts of civic-minded citizens, led by members of the Cultural Heritage Board, it will be preserved. It is one of two buildings in the city listed on the National Register of Historic Places, as it is an outstanding example of Elizabethan Tudor architecture. At one time the famous Lincoln Highway ran in front of this building.

The Franklin School was built in 1859 on Center Street, near Washington Street, the first publicly-owned school in Stockton. As it was located near "Chinatown," it was predominantly attended by Chinese students. The building became a warehouse sometime after 1900 and was torn down in 1959.

Miss Lottie Grunsky.

Lottie Grunsky School was built in 1919 in the 1600 block of East Harding Way and named for a highly respected and loved teacher. In 1977 a new earthquake-resistant school was built behind the old school, which was torn down.

The four-room Weber Primary School was erected in 1873 at 55 West Flora Street. The "new" Franklin School that once stood on Center between Washington and Lafayette Streets had been built from the same plans two years earlier. In recent years the old Weber School was a day care center; it has been restored and now serves as offices for the Multi Lingual-Multi Cultural Center of the Stockton Unified School District.

Speaking at the dedication of the Hoover School on August 30, 1954 is Dr. Robert Burns, president of the College of the Pacific at that time. Other speakers, from left to right, were: Dr. Tully Knoles, College of the Pacific; Warren Atherton and George Ditz, local attorneys; former President of the United States Herbert Hoover; and Cy Owen, principal of the school.

Dr. Joseph Blanchard, President of San Joaquin Delta College from 1969 to 1976.

Aerial view of the San Joaquin Delta College, 1977. The entrance to the campus can be seen in the lower right on Pacific Avenue.

The first graduating kindergarten class of Lincoln School, with their teacher, "Miss Polly," in 1950. The school is at Pacific Avenue and Lincoln Road.

Protest march of students along Weber Avenue in 1910. The unfinished building in the background became the San Joaquin Hotel; today it is "Mexico City Joe's" Restaurant.

The new College of the Pacific campus just after the major buildings had been completed in 1924-1925 and before any landscaping had been started. The building in the center of the picture housed the Conservatory of Music and the auditorium. Pacific has been outstanding for the offerings of the School of Music, including an a capella choir that was started by Dean C. M. Dennis and achieved fame. In the mid-twenties the enrollment at Pacific was around 600. In 1977 there are 5,793 students attending the University at the four different locations.

When the name was College of the Pacific, the Smith Memorial Gate was located on the east side of the campus among the cluster of five valley oaks that had been standing on the land when the college was built.

The beautiful Morris Chapel and Christian Education units, built in 1942 on the campus of the College of the Pacific, were made possible by a gift from Mr. and Mrs. Percy F. Morris. The chapel is used by students of all denominations. During June so many weddings are held there, especially on weekends, that they are often scheduled by the hour. Sunset magazine carried a story on Stockton and was so bold as to state that the Morris Chapel, with its beautiful stained glass windows, was the most important sight to see in Stockton.

The campus of the University of the Pacific, then still the College of the Pacific, c. 1948. This picture was taken before construction of the Irving Martin Library, Grace Covell Dormitory, the Wendel Phillips Center, or any of the cluster colleges.

"Pacific's 'Three Giant Sequoias'" was the caption given this 1954 picture of three great College of the Pacific leaders of the 1940s and 1950s. Left to right are Dr. Rockwell D. Hunt, retired from twenty-five years as Dean of the Graduate School of U.S.C., then director of Pacific's California History Foundation; Amos Alonzo Stagg, retired football coach from the University of Chicago, who coached football at Pacific another fourteen years; and Dr. Tully C. Knoles, president of the college from 1919 to 1946.

On the right is Robert Burns of Richmond, as an undergraduate student at the College of the Pacific in 1929, with two of his friends and fellow students, R. Coke Wood of Bishop, and Elmer Stevens of Nevada City in the center. All three were involved in activities of the campus Y.M.C.A. and participated in debate. This picture was taken on the steps of Anderson Dining Hall, just after lunch. These three college friends all became outstanding California educators.

Dr. Robert E. Burns, who became president in 1947, standing under the memorial gate after the name had been changed to the University of the Pacific in 1960. The tower in the background, now known as the Burns Memorial Tower, houses a 10,000-gallon water tank and the main administrative offices. Built during Burns' administration, it is an example of the kind of innovative approach he often took to problems. He served as president from 1947 until his death in 1971. During those twenty-five years the school expanded and changed more than it had in the previous 100 years.

Dr. Tully Knoles leading the homecoming parade in 1955. This parade had become a tradition over the years and Dr. Knoles loved to show off his horse. He was a familiar sight to the students as he went for his early morning ride around the campus and down the Calaveras River levee.

Dr. Stanley E. McCaffrey became the twenty-first president of the University of the Pacific in the fall of 1971, after the death of Dr. Robert Burns. Under the energetic leadership of President McCaffrey the University has continued to expand and grow. Student enrollment has increased during a period when most colleges and universities have had falling enrollments, and the old San Joaquin Delta campus has been purchased and is being restored and beautified as the new South Campus. The plant today consists of four liberal arts colleges and seven professional schools, in four different locations. In this 126th year since the college was founded, the University had its greatest number of graduates with degrees conferred in eleven separate commencement exercises.

Amos Alonzo Stagg, famous University of Chicago football coach, is greeted by President Tully C. Knoles in 1933 as he arrives in Sacramento. A triumphal caravan drive to Stockton followed this greeting. After retiring from the University of Chicago, Coach Stagg had a second great career at Pacific.

Eddie LeBaron from Oakdale, an outstanding football star, enrolled at the College of the Pacific at age sixteen. He played football in his first year in 1946 with Coach Amos Alonzo Stagg, and with Coach Larry Semmering in '47, '48, and '49. After leaving Pacific he went to George Washington University as a law student. He played professional football with the Washington Redskins and the Dallas Cowboys, and at present is the general manager of the Atlanta Falcons. The above picture was taken in 1949 and was titled "What do good quarterbacks talk about?" Left to right: Bob Wicker, who made a 75-yard touchdown run when playing for College of the Pacific in 1934 against the University of California; Charles "Boots" Erb, famous quarterback from the University of California and an All-American; Eddie LeBaron; and Coach Larry Semmering.

The 1929 football team in the new Baxter Stadium. From left to right are Lloyd Treuman, Harold Chastain, Erwin "Swede" Righter (the coach), Bill King, and Vernon "Pop" Stoultz. In January 1924, when the faculty voted to raise the graduation requirements to 124 units and give physical education academic recognition, "Swede" Righter was employed as director and coach. The new gymnasium was dedicated on January 17, 1925, and Baxter Stadium at Homecoming in 1929.

Chris Kjeldsen, popular swimming and basketball coach at Pacific until his untimely death in 1962. Chris was a Pacific alumnus with a major in physical education. In his undergraduate days he was all-conference tackle on the football team.

The historic Fallon House Theatre, located at Columbia in the Mother Lode near Sonora, was built in the 1850s by Jim Fallon as part of his hotel. In the 1940s it had become so deteriorated that plans were made to dismantle it. Robert Burns learned of its predicament and raised funds for its purchase. When Columbia was made a State Park, Pacific donated the building to the state with the agreement that it could be used as a summer repertory theater for Pacific's drama students. The first performance was in July 1949 as part of the Centennial celebration. Pacific students, directed by DeMarcus Brown, presented the old melodrama, "Under the Gaslight," to capacity audiences for three days. This was the beginning of successful seasons for twenty years for DeMarcus Brown. Since his retirement the Columbia Theatre has continued its popularity under the direction of Dr. Sy Kahn.

DeMarcus Brown, "Marc," started teaching at the College of the Pacific in 1924 and was made head of the "School of Expression." He was in charge of hundreds of theatrical productions until his retirement in 1967, including 360 full length plays. In the twenty years he directed Fallon House Theatre at Columbia State Park, 347 different persons performed in the plays. DeMarcus Brown was instrumental in helping Lois Wheeler, Jo Van Fleet, Darren McGaven, Barbara Baxley, and many others gain fame in films, the theater, and television. During his years at Pacific he founded the Pacific Little Theatre (1924); the Studio Theatre, for student-directed plays (1929); the Outdoor Theatre (1933); the Fallon House Theatre (1949); and the Play Box, an intimate theater (1962).

WEEKLY SAN JOAQUIN REPUBLICAN

VOL. 2.   STOCKTON, CALIFORNIA, SATURDAY MORNING, APRIL 26, 1856.   NO. 23.

Stockton Daily Argus.

VOL. 4.   STOCKTON, CALIFORNIA, FRIDAY MORNING, JANUARY 8, 1858.   NO. 162.

The Evening Mail

LVII.—NO. 151.   STOCKTON, CALIFORNIA, TUESDAY, AUGUST 4, 1908.

MARVELOUS AERIAL FLIGHT

AUTO PLUNGES OVER BLUFF 300 FEET HIGH

Fiery Sea St... in Britis...

11 Communications

Stockton has always been among the leading communities in California in methods of obtaining information for its citizens, with postal service as early as 1849, a newspaper in 1850, telephones in 1881, radio in 1920, and television in 1954.

A good newspaper town from its beginning, Stockton has seen many newspapers come and go. The Stockton *Weekly Times* was first published on March 16, 1850 in a small building at what is now 122 South Center Street. It was an eight-page newspaper, printed on the same little wooden Ramage press that Walter Colton and Robert Semple had used to publish the *Californian*, the first newspaper in California. The *Californian* had originated just four years earlier at Monterey, and lasted only until 1851.

In April 1851, the *Times* was purchased by Captain George Kerr and the name changed to the *San Joaquin Republican*. It became Stockton's first daily newspaper in December 1853. The political sympathies of the newspaper, in spite of its name, were Democratic and during the Civil War it was suppressed by the federal government for printing treasonable editorials. The Stockton *Daily Argus*, organized in 1854, was also suppressed for expressing strong sympathy for the Confederacy.

These newspapers were overshadowed in 1861 by the Stockton *Independent*, which first started as the San Andreas *Independent* in September 1856. This newspaper was politically independent and influential until it ceased publication in 1939.

No effort will be made to list all the newspapers that have been published, for varying lengths of time, in Stockton. However, the most enduring and successful of these has been the Stockton *Record*. Irving Martin, Sr., and William "Pony" Denig began publishing the *Commercial Record* in June 1888. It was located in a basement on Parker's Alley near Hunter Street. The newspaper thrived and in 1895 Martin bought out Denig's interest and changed the name to the Stockton *Record*.

Exchanging facts and fancies, private and public

On April 8, 1895, the first four-page issue of the *Record* was published. When Irving Martin purchased the Stockton *Evening Mail* in 1917, the *Record* obtained a complete monopoly on all wire services into Stockton and has been the dominant newspaper ever since. In May 1952, Irving Martin, Sr., retired after a career of fifty-seven years and turned the office of president over to his grandson, Irving Martin III. After his death, Mrs. Martin sold the newspaper to the Speidel Company, in October 1969. This company operates a chain of newspapers throughout the United States.

Stockton's first postmaster was George Buffum. He opened the first post office on November 8, 1849 in a small "prefabricated" building he had brought with him from Salem, Massachusetts. It was located on the Levee (Weber Avenue), just east of El Dorado Street. The building was used for a grocery and liquor store by the Buffum brothers and only a small space was given to the new post office.

Mail arrived from San Francisco on the river boats and was somewhat uncertain. However, by May 1851 the river steamboating had developed to the point where daily mail replaced the irregular, or semi-weekly, mails from San Francisco. By the summer of 1852, mail became so important that the post office was moved to the first large building in Stockton, the Corinthian, which was located on the north side of Channel Street between El Dorado and Center Streets. At that time, it was discovered that there was a shortage in the accounts of the postmaster, J. G. Candee, and he suddenly left town.

In 1854 a sum of $600 was raised among the businessmen to keep the post office in the center of town. It was moved to the newly built Weber House, on the southwest corner of Main and Center Streets, where it remained for twenty years. No object would be achieved in tracing the various locations of the post offices or listing the many postmasters over the years. However, it might be interesting to point out that the first building expressly constructed as a post office and federal building was erected on the southeast corner of Market and California Streets. The post office was opened there in August 1902. It remained there until a large earthquake-resistant federal building was constructed at San Joaquin and Lindsay Streets at a cost of $670,000. The post office was opened there on March 3, 1933.

Stockton grew and in 1969 the post poffice required more space in an area with less traffic congestion. The main post office was then moved to 4245 West Lane. The 1933 post office remained as one of five branch post offices.

The Mail Building at 29-31 South Sutter Street, about 1901. After the Mail *ceased publication the Stockton* Independent *was published in this building during the 1920s. In later years the ground floor became Ziegler's Billiard Parlor. The upper two stories were removed in the late 1950s and the remainder of the building was torn down about 1970 for a parking lot.*

It would be interesting to note that until 1869, when the Central Pacific Railroad reached Stockton, the city was dependent on the river boats for mail. Although houses and businesses were numbered in 1865, mail was not delivered until the 1890s.

Telephones came to Stockton in 1881, only five years after they had been invented by Alexander Graham Bell. The Stockton Telephone Company was the tenth exchange opened in California. By 1884 the company was owned by the Sunset Telephone and Telegraph Company, which installed a new switchboard and completed the first long distance telephone line from San Francisco to Stockton. Long distance service was soon extended to Sacramento and Marysville.

The first "office," not really a switchboard, was at 127 East Main Street and shared space with other businesses. There were only a few phones and the company had a very small staff. The "business manager" did just about everything—installing phones, repairing, selling, and acting as "Central" (the operator).

The business expanded slowly and at first there was no advantage in owning a telephone as there was practically no one to call. Gradually the advantages of the telephone caught on and by 1892 the company moved into its own building at the southeast corner of San Joaquin and Channel Streets.

The Pacific Telephone and Telegraph Company took over the exchange in 1907. It was moved in 1939 to 345 North San Joaquin Street and a dial system, costing $1,500,000, was put into operation. At that time there were 17,000 subscribers, by 1956 there were 56,275, and in 1977 there are over 75,000 subscribers in Stockton.

Commercial radio came to Stockton very early in the 1920s. The first radio broadcast, giving the results of a presidential election, was in November 1920. It was station KDKA of Pittsburgh, Pennsylvania, broadcasting the Harding-Cox election returns. In 1921, less than two years later, radio station KWG, Stockton's first commercial station, began operating as the Portable Wireless Telephone Company which had been formed by Oard Radio Laboratories of Stockton.

To christen the new station, the great Madame Ernestine Schumann-Heink was brought to Stockton. Her songs were "At Parting" and "The Rosary," after which she went to the Masonic Temple where she gave a concert to a capacity crowd.

The engineer, Paul Oard, who had his laboratory at 1218 North Union Street, designed and built wireless sets for home use before KWG was formed. The call letters were adopted on December 10, 1921. Other commercial radio stations have been formed in Stockton over the years, such as: KGDM, KJOY and KJAX. The University of the Pacific has established a high frequency station, KUOP, as a part of its student training program.

Entrance to the Stockton Record *in the 1920s. People gathered around the loud-speaker to hear the latest results of prize fights, ball games and special events. Note the score board showing Babe Ruth's name (third down on the right). He played for the New York Yankees in the 1923 World Series. Sports reports were relayed to the Stockton* Record *by telegraph and recorded on the board. Although good radio reception was unusual, the reports may have been obtained in that manner at times.*

The Irving Martins, publishers of the Stockton Record. *Seated is Irving Martin, Sr. Standing, right, is his son, Irving Martin, Jr., who wrote the column, "As the Sun Sets." Left is Irving Martin III, known as Gully. The Martins operated the* Record *for sixty-five years.*

The Stockton Daily Record *began in June 1895 on Parker's Alley, off Hunter Street, and moved to its present location on Market Street in 1913. The* Record *now occupies nearly an entire city block on Market Street between California and American Streets.*

Stockton Record *employees at a going-away party for Irvine Sprague in 1956. Mr. Sprague (seated in center) became administrative assistant to Congressman John McFall of Manteca, in Washington, D.C. and later became White House aide under President Lyndon Johnson. In 1968 he became director of the Federal Deposit Insurance Corporation in Washington, D.C. for a six-year period.*

From left to right, seated: Tom Sprague, Herb Stoy, Avery Kizer, Irv Sprague, Mel Bennett, Bill Rogers and Ben Remington. Standing, left to right: Don Drake, Tony Galendo, Harry Mallory, Hank Frosharg, Bob Whittington, Jerry Whitney, Lindsay Campbell and Scott Mathews.

Stockton letter carriers of about 1900. Front row, in uniform, left to right: John Newman, William Elsom, J. S. Burros, Phil Burgess, George Poc, A. E. Eiler. Center row: Postmaster Eli Thrift, John Earl, R. S. Eaten, Hugh Tye, J. Farnsworth. Top row: Railway mail clerk Clark Hall, Miss Myra Ellsworth, Steve Chase. Hugh Tye was later a fireman and a policeman, and for years served as a judicial court judge. Until his death in the 1960s he was known as "Judge Tye."

Stockton's post office, on the southeast corner of Market and California Streets, about 1910. This stone building served as the main post office for more than thirty years. In 1933, as a result of Roosevelt's WPA program, which put unemployed men to work, a large main post office was built at 401 North San Joaquin Streets. The 1902 building became the Hall of Records and was torn down in 1965.

The Christmas mail rush of 1923. The truck is parked beside the 1902 post office at the corner of Market and California Streets.

Below: The post office in 1904. Notice the dress style, spittoons, and combination gas and electric lights.

Pacific Telephone operations and the switchboard operators, c. 1930. In 1939 the exchange moved to new and larger quarters at 345 North San Joaquin Street and the business office was located at 445 North San Joaquin Street. New business offices are now located on Yokuts Avenue in North Stockton.

The Sunset Telephone Company on the southeast corner of San Joaquin and Channel Streets in 1892. It had 351 subscribers. The Pacific Telephone and Telegraph Company took over in 1907. In 1915 Stockton obtained coast-to-coast long distance service.

The flood was nothing to get too excited about; one occurred every few years.

Upstairs at the Stockton Telephone Company, 127 East Main Street, in 1881. Stockton had the tenth telephone exchange in the state. Some of the first subscribers were the Holden Drug Company, the Stockton Savings and Loan Society and the Hoffman Saloon.

Madame Ernestine Schumann Heink dedicates pioneering radio station KWG, in the Stockton Record Building, on November 22, 1921. KWG was one of the nation's earliest radio stations. In 1927 the station moved to the basement of the Medico-Dental Building. In 1930, McClatchy Broadcasting took over, continuing ownership until 1955. The transmitter was located at Weber Avenue and E Street. The station is now located on Robinhood Drive in North Stockton. Church services were first broadcast on Sunday mornings in 1921. On Saturday nights music came from the Dreamland Ballroom. Other memorable broadcasts were of American Legion baseball games and the arrival of the Daisy Gray in 1933, opening the Port of Stockton.

Stockton's first radio car is parked on the Calaveras River Bridge on Lower Sacramento Road, now Pacific Avenue, while a test is conducted. At that time, in the 1920s, this was on the outskirts of town.

This was the first building constructed on the California Street site of the state hospital for the insane. Captain Charles Weber donated 100 acres of land for the hospital and later gave more. This first building, costing $32,000, was completed in 1854.

12 Hospitals

Theaters of the healing arts

It was usually true that during the first few years of the pioneering period of a community, when governmental responsibilities had not been established, the matter of health and care for the ill was a personal and private concern. During the gold rush period in California there were large numbers of gold seekers in the mining areas, but little government, and no hospitals existed for several years. Certain adventurous doctors took time out from their own search for gold to aid the ill or injured, among them Dr. D. J. Locke, founder of Lockeford, but it was not until the 1850s that the stabilized communities had hospitals. These were usually privately owned by an enterprising medical doctor.

As some 350,000 people rushed into California between 1848 and 1851, a great need for hospitals arose. Many men were unable to cope mentally or physically with the rigors and hardships of life in the mines and in the society that had developed around them. The towns of San Francisco, Sacramento and Stockton were unprepared at first to handle either crime or illness. In 1849 San Francisco's town council purchased the abandoned ship *Euphemia* and converted it into a prison ship and hospital for the mentally ill. The brig *Susanne* was similarly used in Stockton.

By 1850, with the organization of state and local governments, the need for hospitals was being recognized. In the next few years, these needs were met by three different bodies: the state government, the county government, and private organizations or individuals.

Stockton experienced a particular need for hospitals and medical care, in its position as a supply base for the Southern Mines and part of the Mother Lode. Three general state hospitals were established by the legislature on April 30, 1851, one to be in Stockton. The other two were located in San Francisco and Sacramento. The Stockton State Hospital admitted both the physically and mentally ill. Dr. Robert K. Reid was selected as the first resident physician (superintendent).

In 1852, as a result of a report that the Sacramento General Hospital was caring for thirty-four insane patients, the legislature created a separate institution exclusively for the mentally disturbed to be located in Stockton as part of the general hospital. Stockton was considered centrally located and the climate was preferred to that of San Francisco.

Captain Weber gave the State one hundred acres for the hospital along California Street, later adding to the acreage. The state provided $10,000 to erect the first building in 1852. Only mentally ill patients were sent to the insane asylum after May 1853, and this institution became the first publicly supported psychiatric facility in the West. By October 1853 all 284 mental patients had been transferred from Center and Market Streets to the California Street site. Also in the same year the name was changed to Insane Asylum of the State of California. Every year from 1854 to 1857 a new wing was added to this facility or a new building constructed. In 1854, because of crowded conditions, the trustees found it necessary to construct a new main building. A contract for $56,666 was awarded to J. J. Dewey.

Other additions were added as required, including wings to the female department in 1865 and 1874. In 1949, this building was dismantled and replaced by several one- and two-story buildings. The male department was built on Grant Street about 1875. After a fire ravaged the south wing in 1938, the top floor was removed. It was replaced after 1958.

By 1880 the number of patients had increased to 1,116 and the institution was badly overcrowded. Efforts were made to establish a state farm and dairy out on the Lower Sacramento Road to relieve the crowding and to provide food for the State Hospital. This was achieved in 1904, other acreage was acquired, and the farm eventually comprised 1,121 acres. About 1,500 patients were transferred there from the downtown facility. By 1953, 4,600 men and women were being cared for at the State Hospital.

Because of the growth of North Stockton and the high cost of operations, phasing out began in 1959 and the last patients were removed in 1968. The 165-acre San Joaquin Delta College campus now occupies the site of the main buildings of the old farm.

Besides the first superintendent, Dr. Robert Reid, the hospital was served by several others of outstanding ability. Dr. George A. Shurtleff was appointed in 1865 and served until 1883. His influence helped create and establish Napa State Hospital, the second in the state for the care of the mentally ill.

Dr. Asa Clark was another of the outstanding superintendents of the hospital. He served from 1892 to 1906. His son, Dr. Fred Clark, held the office for twenty-three years.

Dr. Margaret Smythe served as superintendent from 1929 to 1946. She was the first women superintendent of a mental hospital in the United States, and set an outstanding record in developing new treatments for the mentally ill.

The first San Joaquin County Hospital had its origin in the 1850s, when Dr. E. B. Bateman was allowed $3,400 by the supervisors to operate a pest house for contagious diseases. However, the county hospital and grounds were not established until 1864, when a site was acquired at Wilson Way and Hazelton Avenue and some older buildings were moved onto the grounds. The first new building on this site was constructed in 1879 for $11,000. These buildings were burned in a great fire on June 3, 1892, in spite of the efforts of Stockton's three fire companies. All 140 patients were removed safely and taken to the Pavilion at Washington and Hunter Streets, for temporary care.

After this fire plans were made to move the county hospital to a new site near French Camp. The first buildings there were ready for occupancy in January 1895. Dr. Samuel E. Latta was the first superintendent in charge of the newly relocated hospital. He was replaced in 1902 by Dr. J. D. Dameron, who started a nurses' training school. In 1912, Dr. William Friedberger was appointed superintendent. He held the position for thirty years.

Brick buildings have replaced the first wooden structures. The first brick wing was completed in 1932 and the second in 1943. The present hospital plant consists of twenty-four buildings on a 430-acre site.

There have been a number of private hospitals serving Stockton but the two most significant and historic are St. Joseph's Hospital and Dameron Hospital.

St. Joseph's Hospital was originally founded in 1898 as St. Joseph's Home by Father W. B. O'Connor, a rest home for elderly men. It was located on California and Walnut Streets and also had a hospital annex, which was operated by the Dominican Sisters. At first it had twenty beds and a few doctors. By 1905, the hospital was operating a school of nursing which continued until 1938.

The original two-story brick building was enlarged in 1918 and major additions and wings have since been added. It is now one of the best equipped hospitals with over a hundred doctors serving patients there. It is nonsectarian and the majority of the patients are not Catholic.

Dameron Hospital, Stockton's other modern and well-equipped hospital, was started by Dr. J. D. Dameron in 1912, after he had served as superintendent of the county hospital. It is located on Lincoln and Magnolia Streets and has been greatly expanded by modern buildings and wings that occupy an entire city block. It has some of the latest equipment such as its ten-bed facility for treating burn victims.

The local hospitals were under great strain during the influenza epidemic of 1919 which caused hundreds of deaths and overwhelmed the hospitals with patients. It was caused by a new virus, and wonder drugs such as sulpha, penicillin and antibiotics had not yet been developed. Doctors could only improvise and experiment with treatment. As the infection was highly contagious, public gatherings were discouraged and schools were dismissed in many communities. One of the devices used to prevent the virus from spreading was a gauze mask to be worn over the nose and mouth in public. Today it may seem ludicrous, but in the frightening months of the epidemic it was a desperate effort to control an unknown disease.

Drug stores have always been important in Stockton's medical history and the first one was Holden's Drug Store. It was started by "Doc" Erastus S. Holden, who organized the Holden Drug Company in 1850. After the great fire of 1853, he constructed a two-story, brick, fireproof building on Main and El Dorado Streets in 1854. This store was the oldest brick building in Stockton but its historical importance did not save it from demolition in 1967 during redevelopment of the west end. At a special ceremony, held by the Chamber of Commerce on May 2, 1967, souvenir bricks from the building were sold for one dollar. The profit benefited the California History Foundation at the University of the Pacific.

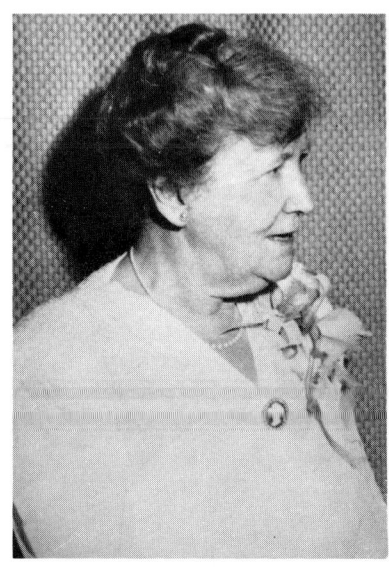

Dr. Margaret Smythe was superintendent of the Stockton State Hospital from 1929 to 1946.

Dr. S. E. Latta was the first medical doctor and surgeon in charge of the county hospital.

Located on a thirty-six-acre site at the northwest corner of Wilson Way and Hazelton Avenue, this was the first building built especially for a county hospital. The hospital can be traced back to 1857, when there were facilities under the direction of Dr. E. B. Bateman, in makeshift buildings in various locations. This building was constructed in 1879 at a cost of $11,000. It burned in 1892.

The first hospital on the present site in French Camp was erected in 1895. A school of nursing was established by the hospital a decade later. The county's hall for dependent children is named for the first graduate nurse, Mary Graham.

The San Joaquin General Hospital in French Camp, 1977. It now has more than 1,000 rooms on a 430-acre site. Approximately 10,000 patients are admitted yearly.

St. Joseph's Hospital was founded in 1898 by Father William B. O'Connor, who spent nearly forty years doing benevolent work in Stockton. The facility has grown steadily over the years, with the latest addition reaching completion in 1970. It is located at California and Walnut Streets.

Father William B. O'Connor, who opened St. Joseph's Hospital in 1898.

Below: St. Joseph's Hospital School of Nursing graduated its first nurses in 1905 and continued offering training until 1938.

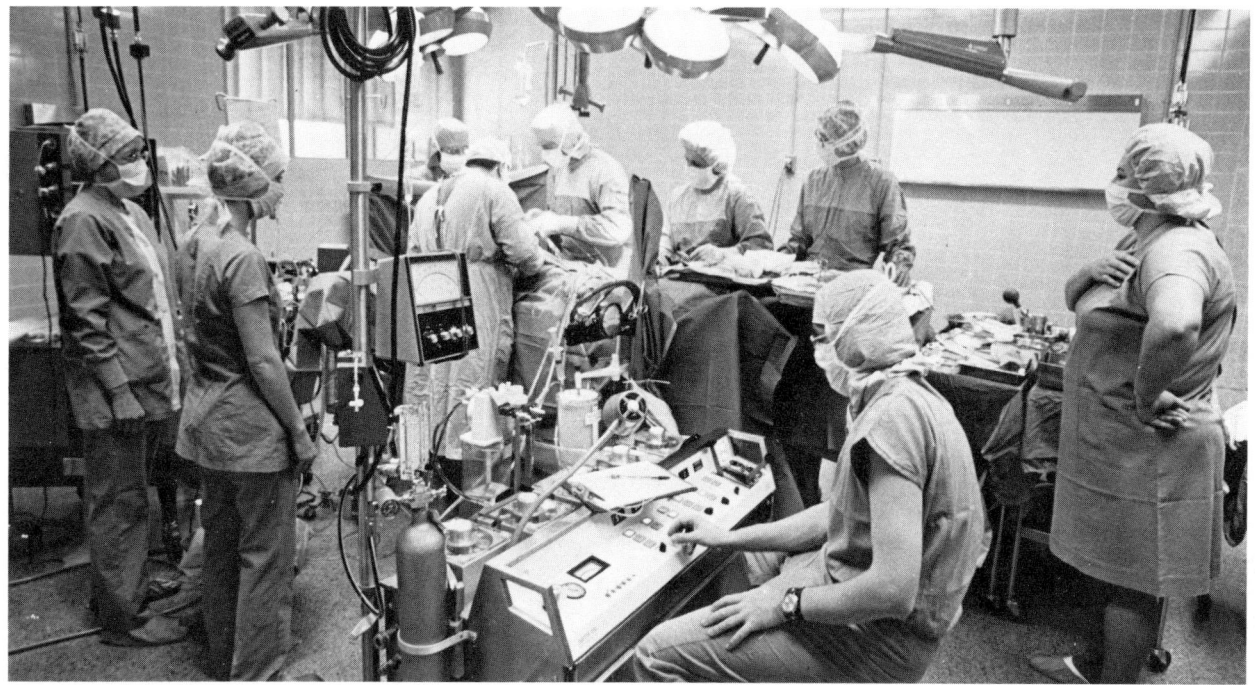

The surgical team at work in St. Joseph's Hospital. In 1975 open heart surgery for valve replacements, coronary bypass, atrial septal defects and trauma was performed on sixty patients.

An air view of St. Joseph's Hospital in 1977. Two hundred and thirty physicians refer their patients to St. Joseph's, which covers a ten-acre area, has 166 rooms, 316 beds, over 1,000 paid employees, and the volunteer services of nearly 700 members of the Women's Auxiliary and Junior Auxiliary.

The Pacific Hospital was built in 1871 by Dr. Asa Clark. It covered forty acres and was the first private institution for the treatment of mental disorders in Stockton. The site is now occupied by Edison High School.

Dr. Asa Clark was in charge of the Stockton State Hospital and later owned and operated the Pacific Hospital and Clark Sanitarium.

Dr. J. D. Dameron was in charge of the county hospital from 1902 to 1912. In 1912 he opened Dameron Hospital.

Dameron Hospital was founded by Dr. J. D. Dameron in 1912. This is the original building, which occupied the southwest corner of Lincoln and Magnolia Streets until just a few years ago.

Dameron Hospital in 1977. A new addition (right corner) has just been completed. The hospital and parking area cover a city block bounded by Lincoln, Magnolia, Acacia and Harrison Streets.

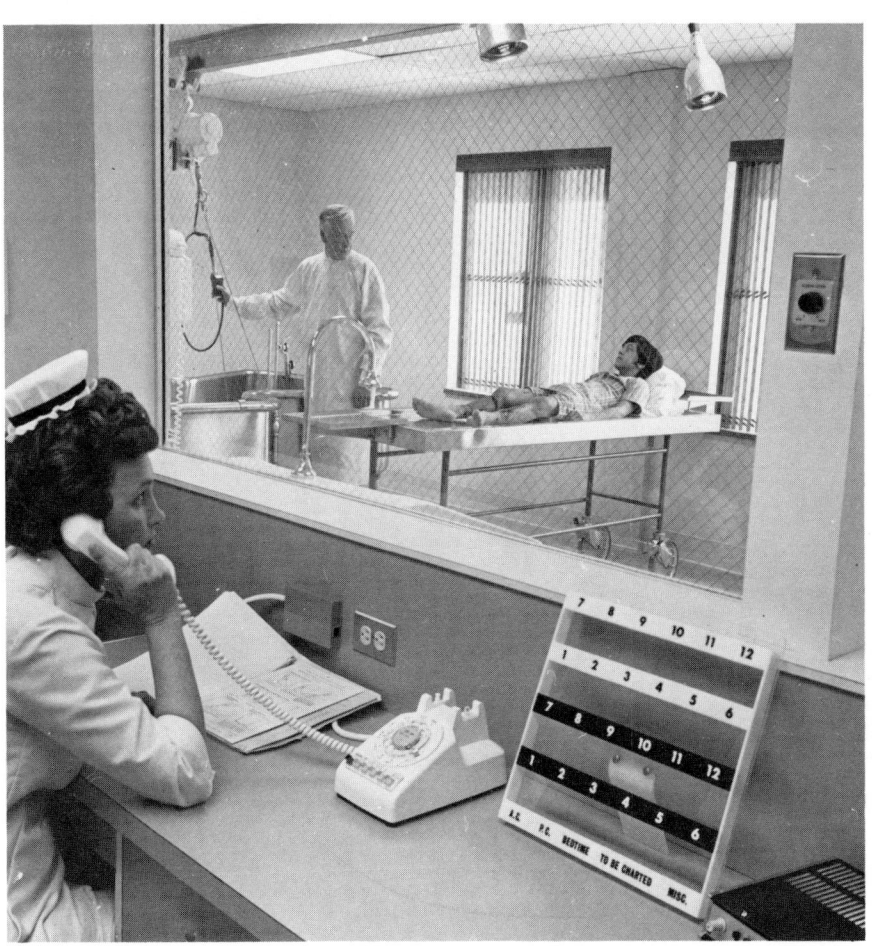

In 1972 Dameron Hospital installed a ten-bed facility with special equipment for the treatment of burn victims. In the same year the hospital announced the installation of a space age air sterilizer to minimize the possibility of infection.

The Owl Drug Store on the northeast corner of California and Main Streets in 1958. It was almost a landmark over the years and is well remembered by old-timers.

Facing page: Interior view of the Holden Drug Store, Main and El Dorado Streets. Since 1919 the store has been known as Forty-Nine Drug Co., Inc. At present the owner is Carl Michelotti, whose father purchased the business in 1947 after being associated with the company since 1929. The new location of the Forty-Nine Drug Store is 947 North Yosemite.

"Doc" Holden (Erastus S. Holden), druggist. He built the first two-story brick building in Stockton, a drug store on the northeast corner of Main and El Dorado Streets. He served as mayor from 1859 to 1862 and was elected again in 1871; he was also active in organizing the San Joaquin Valley Agricultural Society, another of his many public-spirited projects that helped him earn a reputation as an outstanding community leader. Rulers, colorful advertising cards and free samples given away at his drug store also kept his name before the public constantly.

The Holden Drug Company at the northeast corner of El Dorado and Main Streets, as it appeared during the Gold Rush. The first building burned in 1853 and was rebuilt with brick. This building stood until 1967.

Red Cross nurses marching in Hunter Square during the flu epidemic of 1919.

The office staff of the Sperry Flour Company posed outside the mill office during the 1919 flu epidemic. Note the attempts at humor—the man on the far right is wearing an apron; another man in the center has a mask on top of his head.

A parade down Weber Avenue during the great influenza epidemic of 1919. Everyone had to wear masks in public places, although the members of the band were apparently exempt from that rule, at least until their performance was over.

13 Religion

"Peace to all who enter."

Someone has pointed out that if you take the "l" out of gold you have God. This might refer to the experience in California during the gold rush period and it might apply to Stockton. Eager gold seekers rushing to the mining districts had only one thought and that was to get the gold that was said to be so abundant. Families, ideals, customs, and even God were forgotten. But all kinds of men, good and bad, came in search of gold, and they came through Stockton, a jumping off place for the Southern Mines. A great deal has been written about the bad men—the bandits, robbers, ruffians, and gamblers—but the good men came also. The men of God who knew that this new society would need churches and religion also came in search of gold. They soon turned from the quest for gold to a search for souls that would refine this rough society into a great new civilization.

Christian leaders and ministers began holding religious services in tents and even in saloons very early in the gold rush period. The Rev. James C. Damon, a Presbyterian minister, claimed the distinction of conducting Stockton's first church service aboard a ship moored along the levee on July 12, 1849. As ministers of the faith arrived, plans were made to organize churches and raise church buildings.

The Methodists claim the honor of organizing the first church. Elder Isaac Owen was sent to Stockton from San Jose to start a Methodist church in Stockton. It is claimed that when he arrived he heard rumors that the Presbyterians were planning to organize a church on the following Sunday, so he went into immediate action and organized the Methodist Church on March 16, 1850. James Corwin was the first pastor. He was successful in raising $12,000 during the next year to build the first little wooden church building on Weber Avenue and San Joaquin Street.

Later the Methodists bought the brick Agricultural Hall on San Joaquin Street for $22,000 and remodeled it for church purposes. The Rev. Thomas Starr King spoke there on July 4, 1862, giving a marvelous speech urging Californians to remain loyal to the Union. The building served the Methodists well until the 1880s, when it became crowded. Because they also wanted to get away from the congested business center, they purchased a new site at Miner Avenue and San Joaquin Street. On this site was erected the most beautiful brick church in Stockton, the Central Methodist Church, at a cost of $81,000. The first service was held by Pastor S. J. Carroll in 1891.

Time and Stockton's growth had the same effect on this church as on the older one, and by 1958 the congregation needed a new church building away from the downtown traffic and closer to principal residential districts. A new site was acquired across Pacific Avenue from the University of the Pacific, where the modern Central Methodist Church is located.

The Presbyterians were only one day behind the Methodists in organizing a church in Stockton, on March 17, 1850, under the leadership of the miner-minister Rev. James Woods. The first church building constructed in Stockton was built by the Presbyterians on a site donated by Captain Weber on the southeast corner of Main and San Joaquin Streets. The Rev. Woods, using gold dust donated by interested citizens, purchased lumber in San Francisco that had been shipped around the Horn from Massachusetts to use for the building. The cost of the church was $14,000, and a borrowed ship bell was used to call the worshipers together when the building was dedicated on May 5, 1850. It is interesting to note that the first congregation of twelve consisted of eleven men and one woman, Rev. Woods' wife.

This little wooden church was soon outgrown and in 1859 the Presbyterians sold the little wooden building and erected a brick building on the same site, at a cost of $19,000. In order to finance the construction they sold part of the original site given them by Captain Weber and sold pews to the highest bidders. The beautiful new church was dedicated on Christmas Day 1859. Two years later the congregation raised funds for a fine new organ, the largest in Stockton.

The building was enlarged as needed, but by the 1920s the congregation had grown enough that a new edifice was necessary, and a location away from the business district seemed desirable. The lot and building were sold to Smith and Lang for $62,000, and torn down. A new site was obtained at El Dorado and Vine Streets and the present beautiful brick church was built at a cost of $186,000 and dedicated on March 25, 1923.

The Episcopalians were also one of the pioneer churches of Stockton. A small congregation was organized under the leadership of the Rev. Orlando Harriman and the first service was held on August 25, 1850 in the City Hall. The minister soon retired due to ill health, but services continued under the leadership of J. M. Bissell and lay leaders until 1853, when St. John's Church welcomed the Rev. John Reynolds of San Diego as its pastor.

It was during the ministry of Rev. E. Hagar, 1856-1859, that a church building was constructed on two lots donated by Captain Weber on the northeast corner of El Dorado Street and Miner Avenue. This building, costing $10,000, was the first brick church building in Stockton and contained the first pipe organ in the city. It was dedicated on June 22, 1858, with Rev. Hagar presiding.

This building served the congregation until the 1880s when funds were collected for a new church. The first unit was the Guild Hall, a rare example of Nordic architecture, completed in 1889 at a cost of $9,200 and used for church purposes. It is still a source of interest to visitors because of its unique architecture.

The adjacent church building, cruciform in shape, in the style of old English cathedrals, was completed and the first service held there in 1892.

The Catholic Church was one of the pioneer congregations organized in 1850 in Stockton, although Catholic mass had been held in 1849 in Captain Weber's home by two priests on their way to the mines. The congregation was organized in a private home in December 1850, but no regular priest served the church until 1851, when Father Dominic Blaive came through Stockton on his way to the mines and learned that the church had no leader. He agreed to serve temporarily as parish priest, but actually remained three years.

Captain Weber did as he had done with the other pioneer churches, and gave the parish two lots at Washington and Hunter Streets.

The first church building, a wooden structure, had limited seating, but by 1860 the Catholics had collected enough funds to plan a new brick church, the old St. Mary's Church of today, and the cornerstone was dedicated July 21, 1861 by Archbishop Alemany, California's first Archbishop. By Christmas the new $30,000 building was completed and a great crowd came out to hear Father Joseph Gallagher conduct Christmas Eve mass.

In May 1862 the first third of the planned church building was consecrated by Archbishop Alemany. In 1870 an addition to the north of the building was com-

The Methodist Church on the east side of San Joaquin Street between Main and Weber Avenue. The building was originally the Agricultural Hall used by the District Fair Association. After completing a huge church building at San Joaquin and Miner Avenue in 1891, the Methodists sold their original property to the First National Bank.

pleted and work on the third part of the church was started. The organ loft was rebuilt and the baptistry, sacristy, and side chapel were finished. The impressive Gothic spire was erected in 1893. The building was remodeled again between 1945 and 1949 under the direction of Father W. E. McGough. In 1951 the centennial of the church was observed and old St. Mary's Church was claimed to be the third oldest church in Central California.

As women and children came to California a need for schools and churches came with them, and during the 1850s many churches were organized in Stockton. Today almost all denominations are represented here and here are many fine church buildings.

The Rev. Isaac Owen came to Stockton early in the Gold Rush and founded the Methodist Church, the first church established in Stockton.

The choir section and pipe organ of the Central Methodist Church. The building was completed in 1891.

The sixty-seven-year-old Central Methodist Church as it looked when farewell services were held on July 20, 1958 by the Rev. George Goodwin. It was sold to the Bank of Stockton. The stained glass windows were put in the new church on Pacific Avenue and Fulton Street.

First Congregational Church was built in 1869 and was located on Miner Avenue between Sutter and San Joaquin Streets.

The Rev. Reubin H. Sink was pastor of the First Congregational Church for several decades, starting in 1889. While he was pastor a major building program was completed and an excellent reputation for music was established by the church.

The Presbyterian Church on San Joaquin Street between Market and Main Streets in the 1860s. The first Presbyterian services were held in the Mt. Vernon House on Weber Point in 1850. In the same year a wooden church was erected on San Joaquin Street, and in 1859 a new church was erected on the southeast corner of San Joaquin and Main Streets. This building was rebuilt in 1855. In 1922 ground was broken for the construction of the beautiful red brick Presbyterian Church on the northwest corner of El Dorado and Vine Streets, the site of the original wooden El Dorado School.

The Rev. James Woods founded Stockton's first Presbyterian church in 1850.

Reverend Donald R. Latimer was pastor of the East Side Presbyterian Church and one of Stockton's most popular ministers. Known and respected by hundreds of local people, he was honored with a recognition dinner in 1966. Just two years later he died, ending a remarkable record of thirty-three years as a Stockton religious leader.

A golden hand pointing to the heavens from the spire was a special feature of the First Baptist Church at the northwest corner of San Joaquin and Hunter Streets. At the time the building was erected in 1860, at a cost of $16,000 including the lot, the church had a membership of 173. It had been started in 1853 in Rev. J. B. Saxton's house on Sutter Street. Remodeling in 1906 greatly changed the appearance of the building.

One of the oldest church buildings in the city is St. John's Episcopal Church on the northeast corner of El Dorado Street and Miner Avenue. This is the second house of worship built by the Episcopalians; the first, built in 1858, was on the same site. The present building, dating from 1892, contains the original organ and stained glass chancel window from the earlier church. This is just one of a series of stained glass windows throughout the edifice. The Guild Hall, to the right, dates from 1889.

St. Mary's Catholic Church at 214 East Washington Street. This picture was taken about 1890, before the Gothic steeple and facade were added. The first known Catholic Mass in Stockton was at Captain C. M. Weber's home in 1849.

The Jewish Synagogue, on Hunter between Lindsay and Fremont Streets, was built in 1905. The first Jewish congregation was organized in 1855 and led by Rabbi Ackermann. Temple Israel Cemetery, located on Acacia at Union Street, occupies a square block of land donated by Captain Weber in 1851. It is the oldest Jewish cemetery in continuous use west of the Rocky Mountains.

14 Entertainment

Entertainment in Stockton, over the years, has included a wide range of activities. To see when, where and how people played is always fun, and the scenes that follow, though limited, tell an interesting story.

From Stockton's earliest days, the miners going to and from the mines came to the young town for supplies and for fun, especially after striking it rich. Records indicate that the saloon was the chief house of entertainment during the gold mining period. Drinking, gambling, and patronizing saloon girls were the main activities. These forms of entertainment were available in Stockton for many years, even up until modern times.

The "Oldest Profession" was a very important part of Stockton's entertainment picture. Hundreds of men, rushing to the mines for gold, were hungry for even a look at a woman. Prostitution with "cribs," Bull Pens and red light sections were an important part of Stockton life until after World War II.

The theatre has also been a significant part of Stockton's cultural activity, starting in gold rush days. All famous traveling entertainers found Stockton a good town for drama, music and dancing during the early period. Among them were Edwin Booth, Shakespearean actor; Lotta Crabtree, the famous child entertainer; and Maude Adams and Blanche Bates, well-known actresses. Maguire's California Minstrels performed more than once to an enthusiastic audience.

Important theaters, over the years, were the Stockton, opened in 1853 at the corner of Main and El Dorado Streets; the Avon, opened in 1882; and the Yosemite, built in 1892 and located on San Joaquin Street between Weber Avenue and Main Street. When John C. Fremont was operating his rich gold mine near Mariposa, he and his wife, Jessie, would drive to Stockton to attend the Stockton Theater.

Many theaters were started after motion pictures were introduced to Stockton. In the 1920s, with a population of 56,000, the Stockton community had at least twenty movie theaters and three or four vaudeville

"All work and no play. . ."

houses. Today, with a population of 120,000, there are less than a dozen.

The period of the 1920s and 1930s is known as the golden age of motion pictures. New inventions, such as sound pictures and wide screens, were developed. It was a period of great and gaudy theater buildings, the most elaborate of which was the Fox California. Cecil B. DeMille was producing spectaculars such as *King of Kings*, which brought out large crowds to fill motion picture palaces such as the Fox on Main Street, which will soon be restored.

Many important movies were filmed in Stockton during these years, such as Will Rogers' *Steamboat 'Round the Bend*, *Blood Alley*, *Our Miss Brooks*, *Big Country*, *God's Little Acre*, *The Jack Knife Man*, *Cool Hand Luke*, *Oklahoma Crude*, and *Fat City*. Several TV pilot films were also made here, including "Little House on the Prairie," "Happy Days," and "Man Hunters." The importance of the Stockton area to the movie industry is reflected by the fact that the Greater Stockton Chamber of Commerce has one of the few movie promotion offices in the United States outside of Hollywood.

Strong local interest in drama resulted in the formation of the Stockton Civic Theater in 1950. Its first production was *Our Town*, at Madison School Auditorium. This theater has been very successful in bringing outstanding productions to appreciative Stockton audiences. It was also in the 1950s that a Stockton girl, Janet Leigh, became a famous movie star.

The circus and circus parades have always thrilled Stockton audiences and several circus companies have used Stockton for their winter quarters. The Sells Floto Company used the county fair grounds as its winter training base for several years.

As early as 1850, W. H. Foley's one ring of well-trained horses from San Jose performed in front of the Stockton House. They were so popular that they remained longer than originally scheduled.

Parades were always a part of the circus excitement, but there were other parades in Stockton too, such as those on July 4th and in connection with other special events. When the Delta was a large potato growing area, "Potato Day" was celebrated in Stockton with parades and exhibits. Luther Burbank, the famous horticulturist, was a special guest of Mayor Oullahan at the "Potato Day" celebration one year because of his success in growing a new and improved potato.

There were a number of baths, both outdoors and indoors, such as Jackson's Baths, now McKinley Park. Yosemite Lake was a popular unsupervised swimming hole, as was Malibu Beach, several miles down the Stockton Channel.

Many forty-niners were talented musicians and organized bands. Starting in the Mother Lode country, they would often come to Stockton to entertain in the Hunter Square Plaza. The Murphys Cornet Band was the favorite.

Concert music became popular in Stockton soon after the turn of the century. The Zallo Family, a quartet composed of a cello, viola and violins, performed in Stockton for years. In 1902 the Musicians Union Local 189 was formed. Beginning in 1918, dance bands began to organize in Stockton. In the 1920s the favorite dances were the Turkey Trot, Ballin' the Jack, and the Charleston. Some of the public dance halls operating at that time were the Dreamland, Cinderella, Roberts Island Farm Bureau Hall, the Portuguese Hall in Manteca, and the Coconut Grove near Manteca.

Many local bands were playing for dances in the Mother Lode. Some of the bands were Patton and Springer, Polly Watson, Caviglia's Night Hawks, and Tom Castle and his Family Orchestra. Many local musicians joined the big dance bands—Benny Goodman and his Orchestra, Paul Whiteman, Abe Lyman, Harry James, and others. Some Stockton musicians became dance band leaders, among them Gil Evans. One who became world renowned was Dave Brubeck. Some of the night clubs featuring local musicians for dancing and floor shows were the Cotton Club, Club Lido, Plymouth Rock, Marengo's, Mattie's, The Pelican Club, and Matteoni's on North California Street.

Stockton was a great town for dancing, band concerts, night club entertainment and vaudeville shows from the 1920s through the 1950s, but this era has come to an end as old-timers remember it. The big bands were cut to small combos, playing weekends only, and floor shows lost attendance. All this was due to large television audiences. People stayed at home.

Today Stocktonians are still dancing to many fine rock groups. We have an active opera and ballet association. Outstanding music majors are graduating from the University of the Pacific every year, and our Stockton Symphony Orchestra has established a fine reputation.

Maude Adams, who opened the Yosemite Theater on July 12, 1892 with Lost Paradise.

The Yosemite Theater building was located on the east side of San Joaquin Street between Main and Weber. The poster marks the main entrance.

The lobby of the Fox-California Theater, which is still operated at 242 East Main Street. The ornamentation is typical of the entire theater. When it opened on October 3, 1930, 20,000 people hoped to attend one of the initial performances. As the theater capacity was 2,170, fewer than 5,000 were able to gain admittance to the two shows scheduled that day.

The theater was built not only for motion pictures but also to handle the largest traveling road shows. Extensive areas under the stage were partitioned for a chorus room, musicians' rehearsal hall, and dressing rooms. The stage was seventeen feet nineteen inches across and thirty feet deep. A $40,000 Wurlitzer pipe organ was once in the orchestra pit.

The site of the Fox-California was originally occupied by the T and D Theater, built in 1916 and later leased to the Fox West Coast. It was remodeled in 1924, renamed the California and in 1929 was leveled to make way for the new "showplace."

Nearly 2,000 people attended Maude Adams' performance opening the new Yosemite Theater in 1892. This photo shows the interior of the Yosemite in about 1906. Performers who later appeared here were Madjeska, Ann Held, Blanche Bates, Sophie Tucker, Lillian Russell, John Philip Sousa, "Dan and Warfield," Will Rogers, and many more. Later the theater became the Yosemite-Orpheum, then the State, and finally the Esquire, with the entrance changed to Main Street. (Collection of Pioneer Museum & Haggin Galleries, Stockton)

Local youngsters pose for a picture in front of the backdrop of the old State Theater. The young lady with the harp is Edith Dunne White; the others are unidentified. The State played five acts of vaudeville three times a day, with a movie, cartoon, and a newsreel. Manlio Silva led the band in the orchestra pit. The State was the first theater in Stockton to show a sound film, The Jazz Singer with Al Jolson, but the captions were written out and only the singing was in sound. The first complete sound film by Al Jolson was The Singing Fool. The theater was packed at every performance and people could be heard sobbing during the singing of "Sonny Boy."

The Stockton Symphony Orchestra was founded by Manlio Silva, its first music director and conductor. As the early box office returns were small, Mr. Silva would at times pay the musicians from his own pocket. He died in 1958. The Stockton Symphony, directed and conducted by Dr. Kyung Soo-Won, celebrated its fiftieth anniversary in 1977.

Avon Theater building, located on the southeast corner of Main and California Streets. The theater occupied the two upper floors. It opened August 15, 1882 with the play Hazel Kirke. The entrance was to the extreme right on California Street. This building, now remodeled, still stands today.

The Stockton Theater, located on the southeast corner of Main and El Dorado Streets, was built in 1853. This was one of the pioneer theaters where Lotta Crabtree, Edwin Booth and other early-day entertainers performed. The 500-seat theater burned to the ground on July 4, 1890. One of Stockton's earliest known theaters was called "El Placer." It cost $60,000 and opened in 1851 above a saloon on the corner of Weber Avenue and Center Street. It burned about three months later.

A scene from the Civic Theater production of Mr. Roberts in 1955. The Civic Theater was born in the minds of J. Frank Jones, Gail (Scheere) Gott, William E. Appel, Arthur Duning, Lillian Honeychurch, and Clyde Nielson, in the fall of 1951. In 1962 they purchased the old Zion Lutheran Church on the corner of Willow and Monroe Streets. The purchase was made possible by the moral and financial support of long time Civic Theater patrons and donors. The opening of the 197-seat theater was a gala event. The Miracle Worker was the first play performed there. The theater group bought the old Temple Israel Annex on the corner of Madison and Willow Streets, just a block away from the theater. It is used for meetings, rehearsals and storage.

The Sierra Theater at 520 East Main Street in 1953. Stockton had many theaters in the early years of moving pictures, among them the Rialto, State, Strand, Lincoln, Lyric, Ritz, National, and Mandarin.

The Esquire Theater at Main and American Streets. This scene shows people lined up for nearly a block waiting to see (and hear!) Francis, the Talking Mule, in Francis Goes to West Point.

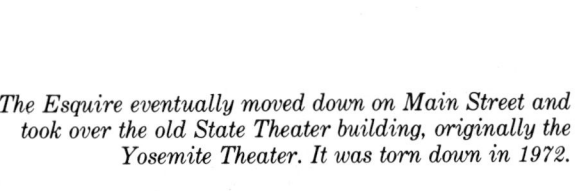

The Esquire eventually moved down on Main Street and took over the old State Theater building, originally the Yosemite Theater. It was torn down in 1972.

Stockton river boats line up for a race featured in the movie Steamboat 'Round the Bend. *Will Rogers played the leading part. Hundreds of local people were hired for the filming of this 1935 movie. Even earlier,* The Jack Knife Man *was made at Dad's Point (Louis Park) by King Vidor. Even William S. Hart made a movie in Stockton in the 1920s.*

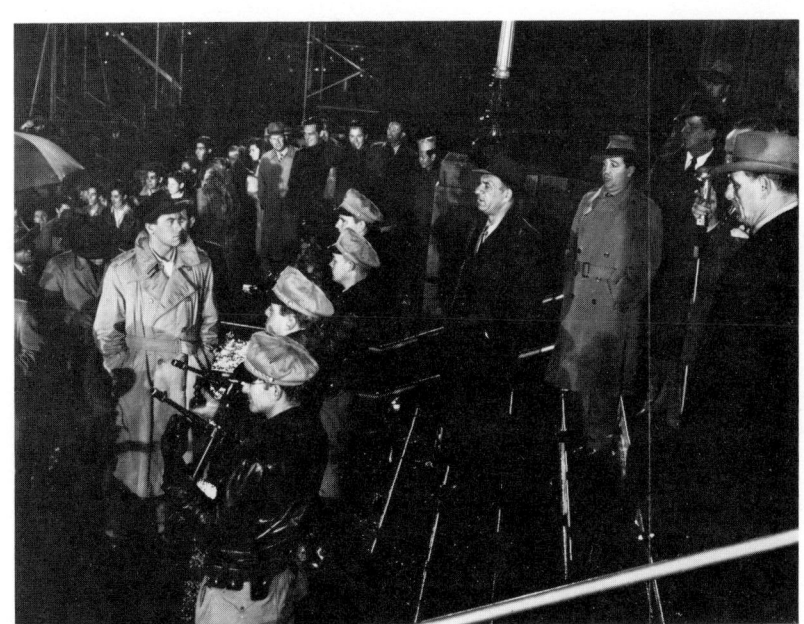

In 1946 All the King's Men, *an academy award winning movie starring Broderick Crawford, was produced here. This scene is on the steps of City Hall and shows co-star John Ireland standing in front of police officers.*

In the early 1950s the movie industry came out with the wide screen. Here a local theater owner compares it with a television set in the lower left-hand corner.

Frank Thornton Smith was best known for the "Monday Nighters," a singing group he formed in 1918. All of the original members were employees of the Holt Manufacturing Company. Smith directed this group continuously until his death at eighty years of age in 1973. The singing group is still active under the direction of Randy Ribarsky.

Dave Brubeck is a world renowned pianist, known for his progressive jazz. He started his career in Stockton at the College of the Pacific in the early 1940s.

Luther Burbank was a guest of Stockton in the 1924 Potato Day parade. Seated to the right of Burbank is then mayor Alex Oullahan.

Circus parade at El Dorado and Main Streets. The circus grounds in the 1920s and 1930s were either on the northeast corner of Main Street and Wilson Way or out on South San Joaquin Street. Later they were on North California Street. In recent years the only circus in Stockton is the Shrine Circus, held at Civic Auditorium.

The Mineral Baths were located at the end of South San Joaquin Street. There were 150 dressing rooms. Children could swim all day for fifteen cents, which included a private dressing room, swim suit and towel. The baths had a club house, scenic railway, merry-go-round, band concerts, barbecue pits, picnic tables, and tennis courts. This was the place to go in the '20s and '30s.

The Mineral Baths were first called the Jackson Natural Gas Well Baths in 1893; later they were called the Mineral Baths and Municipal Baths, and are now McKinley Park and Pool. The Olympic Baths were at Aurora and Fremont and were closed by 1940. The first known baths in Stockton were the Weber Gas Well Baths, built in 1883 on the corner of El Dorado and Weber, now the site of the Hotel Stockton. The Weber Baths, supplied from natural gas wells, had iron, sulphur, soda, and salt. The water was heated and the temperature was always at 85 degrees.

Malibu Beach was the name given to a popular but disreputable area along the Stockton Channel in the 1920s and 1930s. As there were no sanitary facilities or lifeguards on duty, the beach was eventually closed. For many Stockton youngsters it was the "Ol' Swimmin' Hole."

The north bank of Yosemite Lake in 1932. Everybody would swim out to the raft in the center of the lake. Eventually the lake was closed by health authorities after some serious accidents.

Bohemian Bar, 118 South California Street. Notice the spittoons and the bar towels for men to wipe beer suds off their mustaches.

Most early saloons had a painting of a nude woman above the bar.

"Googie and his Dragons," a popular Stockton orchestra, played nightly at Matteoni's night club. From left to right: Al Kech, piano; Vincent "Googie" Richetti, leader and drums; Ernie Massei, saxophone, violin and vocalist; Roland Monteverdi, accordian. This picture was taken in the 1940s.

Matteoni's, Stockton's finest night club, opened at 230 North California Street in 1936. This was a beautiful room for dining, dancing, and terrific floor shows.

In the 1940s and 1950s, elaborate cocktail lounges, such as the Pump Room, 222 North Sutter Street, were springing up all over Stockton.

Welcome to our County

We don't brag about it, but this happens to be a wide open place. Not many like it, anywhere.

FUN AS YOU FIND IT IS OUR GUARANTEED AND PROTECTED BRAND OF HOSPITALITY

Everything's Set--No Embarrassments

If you're a stranger here this partial list may help to guide you: (If you don't know the way, just ask any "wise guy")

THE GEM — (At the sign of the milk bottle.) See Gus, the Dancing Dervish from Tracy in his Famous Enforcement Act. Reputed to have square dice.

THE COOL SHADE—Pretty girls and good eats. Plenty action if you like to shoot craps. What could be lovlier?

THE TAVERN—At the sign of The Cleaners. Everything goes. What more could you ask when properly cleaned?

BEA'S PLACE—See the girl with the Peerless Personality. No law is stronger than her word. You're as safe here as in the cradle.

THE ORO—Bea owns it; the same goes here except for the Personality part of it.

FRENCH'S—Principally eats but no limitations.

STELLA'S—Chickens (both varieties) a specialty.

CHLORINDA'S—She figures the poor must drink as well as live—hence 2-bits a shot.

THE FROG FARM—See the little frogs put on their circus. This is just for the boys.

LOUISA'S — One of those nice chummy dancing resorts.

PERRY'S—Beer with authority.

CHESTER'S—Africa's finest; everything shady.

SANTA FE CAFE—Outside of the proverbial "Chinaman's Chance," you get nothing else in this joint, unless you're lucky, except good music and the usual entertainment.

THE BLACK CAT — You'll find everything here.

MARIPOSA INN — Just ordinary, might drop in if you're passing.

WASHINGTON HOUSE — Good beer. Fine for matinees.

JIMMY DE'S PLACE—Chummy; you'll be satisfied here.

FIVE MILE HOUSE—Not much on entertainment, but a good place to stop when thirsty.

OTTO'S PLACE — Same sort of a place.

FLORINE'S—If you're hungry for a friendly smile drop in here.

THE CHATEAU—Excellent meals besides all the rest.

ANN'S PLACE — Bea's sister. You can expect the same here.

BONNER'S—A regular place; run by a regular guy.

CHARLIE'S PLACE — The Big Fellow and his crowd like to eat here because it's on "the house." Don't let that stop you if you like congeniality. Don't let a "knock-over" or two worry you, because it is only done for effect.

This is but a partial list. There are others, no doubt, but they have not entered into the agreement of "Non-molestation," so anywhere else you may happen to roam might cause a bit of embarrassment. Consequently, we suggest that you find your pleasure where there will be no interruption. As others come into the fold we will issue subsequent bulletins, similar to this.

If everything is not as represented in the above, you'll be doing a favor by reporting the same to the undersigned.

K. K. K.

Posters like this were placed all over town in the 1920s. This was the prohibition era, hence the many references to thirst.

All that remained of a Chinese hotel that was formerly a part of the Bull Pen on Market Street, during the process of demolition in 1966. The cribs could not be seen until the hotel was torn down during redevelopment of the area.

Stockton prostitutes just before the turn of the century. They worked on the south side of Market Street between El Dorado and Hunter Streets. The area was called the Bull Pen, and the rooms were called cribs.

Weber Point in 1900. Captain Weber's original home, built in 1850, is the low two-story building in the center foreground. This home was partially destroyed by the flood of 1890, and shortly thereafter the Webers built the Victorian home next door to the right. That home later became the residence of their daughter, Julia. Shortly after this picture was taken it was moved to West Lane, just north of the Calaveras River. It now belongs to Mrs. Gerald Kennedy, granddaughter of Captain Weber.

Charles M. Weber, founder of the city of Stockton. This picture was taken at his wedding with Helen Murphy in San Jose in 1850. They had three children, Charles M., Jr., Thomas, and Julia.

Charles M. Weber III, founder of Weberstown, poses under the entrance to the Mall in 1960. Weber, a civil engineer, is the grandson of the founder of Stockton and now lives in Austria.

15 Et Cetera

Captain Weber, sports, floods, and more

At the completion of the first fourteen chapters of *Stockton Memories*, two conditions are apparent.

The first is that a number of photographs that should be in the book have not quite belonged in any chapter. Among these are some of Charles M. Weber, whose place of significance in Stockton's history is undebatable. Although he is mentioned in almost every other chapter, he should have a page to himself.

Some of these photographs are of Stockton's dramatic floods, which have so influenced life in this area. Some are of sports figures, some of people who did important and interesting deeds, some of people who had a quarrel with society.

The second noticeable condition of the book at this juncture is that several more chapters would be required to cover every possible topic. One is helpless to avoid the necessary omissions in a book of this kind. There have been so many people, well-known and not-so-well-known, whose lives have influenced the shaping of this city. So many events, notable and not-so-notable, have left their mark in one way or another on the days and years that have followed.

The question of "orphan" photographs has been answered by the addition of this final section, but there is not such a good answer to the problem of unavoidable omissions—perhaps the best answer is the promise of another book some day.

Coxey's Army of unemployed men on board a barge being towed to San Francisco in 1893. They had camped at Banner Island the night before, after marching from Sacramento. Sheriff Cunningham received praise for his prudent handling of these radical demonstrators; after providing food and lodging he put them on a riverboat for San Francisco.

In 1914, the Merchants, Manufacturers and Employers Association tried to break up union activity in Stockton. This resulted in a dispute and demonstrations. More than 2,000 union men took part in this parade. Although the M.M. & E. failed to destroy unionism in Stockton, they managed to weaken it severely.

In the 1960s, the protest march was a way of life, and everyone seemed to be demonstrating for some cause. These marchers on Weber Avenue in 1965 were part of a nationwide protest over civil rights violations in Selma, Alabama.

Stockton flood of 1893. This scene shows the Stockton Channel from atop the county courthouse. The buildings in the lower right were torn down at the start of the construction of the Hotel Stockton.

The Ku Klux Klan lining up for a parade on West Weber Avenue on July 14, 1919. In Stockton, and the nation, the Klan was preaching one hundred percent Americanism, the evils of liquor, Communism, minority races, and the Catholic Church. It should be noted, however, that the Klan was not a violent organization in Stockton. By 1924 it seemed to have died out locally. The last news of the group in San Joaquin County was on May 3, 1940, when the Stockton Record carried a picture of hooded Klansmen holding a night meeting somewhere in the county. The war and tax trouble served as effective dampers on Klan activity in Stockton.

This view of the 1955 flood was taken about eight miles south of the city. Law enforcement agencies had to evacuate hundreds of people from their homes and ranches. The Civic Auditorium was used as a service center, and with the help of the Red Cross, Salvation Army, and other charitable organizations, food, medicine, and beds were provided for the homeless. The downtown area was surrounded by sandbags, but the flood waters never reached it.

The Stockton flood of 1907. This is the intersection of California and Channel Streets, and the horsecar is arriving from the railroad depot to bring guests to the Grand Central Hotel. The rates were $1.25 a day, and the hotel catered mostly to show people. Stockton had a flood almost every year, but some years were worse than others.

One of the worst floods in Stockton history was the flood of December 1955, when all roads leading in and out of the city were closed except Highway 50, and even it was threatened for a while. The airport was closed, railroad tracks were washed out, and most city streets were under water. Mormon Slough had carried nothing more than a trickle of water for over thirty years, but in 1955 it was no different from the rest—none of the streams or rivers could handle the deluge of water. Damage was estimated at $1,700,000 in the city alone. Although dozens of injuries were reported, there was only one death. The statewide loss was $25 million. It was not a merry Christmas.

Residence and Garage.

The Hillman-Rindge mansion on the southwest corner of Harding Way and El Dorado Streets will be remembered by most former Stockton High School students. It was built in 1905 by Frank Hillman and was later owned for many years by Fred Rindge, land developer and mining man. The palatial home had a ballroom and a private carriage drive which went through the grounds—the grandest of the many beautiful homes built along El Dorado Street between 1890 and 1910.

The "Tin Villa," located on the east side of B Street between Sonora and Church Streets, was owned by Joe Prinze, who had an unusual collection of junk all around his property. Kids of the 1920s would throw more junk and "run like sixty!"

Hickinbotham Bros., now in its fifth generation, is still in business on South Aurora Street. The founding brothers, John and Edwin, started their wagon and carriage business on Main Street in 1866. By 1885 the firm had doubled in size, and eleven years later it changed from carriage making to importing and selling hardwood and wagon parts. After forty-two years on Main Street at 269-271, Hickinbotham moved to East Market Street in 1908 where it dealt in heavy hardware and steel jobbing as well as wagon parts and other hardware. During World War II they teamed with Guntert and Zimmerman to produce 176 vessels for government contracts totaling eleven million dollars. The fourth generation is in charge today with Ralph W. as president and his cousin Donald E. as vice president.

The Stone Pine tree on Eugenia Street was grown from seed brought from Italy by Swiss-born Vincent Galgiani. He settled in Stockton in the 1850s, became a farmer and later had extensive business interests, including a fish market and two hotels, the Russ House and the Grand Central. The tree shown here is one of the last reminders of the extensive grounds of Galgiani's "Helvetia Gardens." Vincent Galgiani was the great-grandfather of well known local artist, Oscar Galgiani.

Commodore Robert Field Stockton was Commander of the Pacific Fleet in 1846, and as military governor directed the conquest of California in 1846-1847. He was greatly admired by Captain Charles Weber, the founder of Stockton, who named the city in his honor.

J. D. Peters was born in Genoa, Italy, July 25, 1827, and arrived in Stockton in 1853. He died in his home at 1043 North El Dorado Street on May 27, 1907. Mr. Peters is best known as a grain dealer, but he also had interests in banks, railroads, shipping and other enterprises that helped to build Stockton. He lent financial support to the Masonic hall, the Yosemite Building, and the Yosemite Hotel. He was president of the California Navigation and Improvement Company, and its best steamer, the J. D. Peters, was named for him in 1889. He acted as Grand Marshal of the 1876 Centennial celebration.

One of Peters' unique enterprises was production of an insecticide known as Buhach. Made from a plant, Buhach was first introduced into this country in 1877, and was popular for many years. As a horticulturist Peters won fame throughout the state, especially in the treatment and cultivation of vines and the raising of grapes. He was an authority in many areas. With justice it may be said that no other citizen ever lived in Stockton who labored more earnestly for its prosperity or identified himself more intimately with its industry than J. D. Peters.

John H. "Jack" Tone was a prominent Stockton area farmer. He came to California in 1849 from New York and purchased farm land in 1850. Later he added to it and became a leading grain and cattle rancher in the area. The Tone home, left, is on Jack Tone Road about five miles east of Stockton. This road runs north and south between Ripon and Lockeford. Built in 1873, the house is one of the most interesting old ranch homes in the county.

R. G. LeTorneau invented and manufactured land leveling and road grading equipment. In the early 1920s he started his plant in Stockton at 1615 East Roosevelt (at Wilson Way) and eventually became internationally famous for his machinery.

V. Covert Martin was a noted Stockton photographer and author of the rare historical book Stockton Album Through the Years. *Mr. Martin was a commercial photographer from 1899 until his retirement in 1960. He preserved many of the earlier pictures of Stockton by copying them for his collection. These have been given to the Pioneer Museum and Haggin Galleries, and the Stuart Library at the University of the Pacific.*

John Pitcher Spooner, famous Stockton photographer, poses with his oversize studio portrait camera in 1892. He opened his studio on Main Street in the early 1870s; many of the best surviving historical pictures of Stockton were made by him. He recorded the graduating classes and took portraits of hundreds of early residents. The Spooner Studio was located on the top floor of the Yosemite Building on San Joaquin Street, immediately east of the courthouse. (See page 6.) Some of Spooner's descendants still reside in Stockton.

Left, Mike DeYoung, mortician, businessman, political leader, and highly respected leader of the Knights of Columbus. Right, Ben Wallace, mortician, businessman, Past Master of the San Joaquin Lodge #19 F. & A.M. as a 32nd degree Scottish Rite Mason, and a prominent member of the Central Methodist Church. Both of these men were active in their careers and in community involvement from the 1920s to the 1960s. The families operating DeYoung Memorial Chapel and B. C. Wallace Mortuary have been in the business since the 1890s. In 1977, C. K. "Bud" DeYoung and B. C. Wallace, Jr., are continuing the family firms.

Past presidents of the Stockton Rotary Club, from left to right standing: Frank Zeigler, Hal Barnett, William Inglis. Seated: Dr. Dewey Powell and Bill Kiechler. They were honored by the club at a December 7, 1966 meeting.

Warren Atherton, National Commander of the American Legion, shakes hands with President Franklin D. Roosevelt about 1944. Mr. Atherton, known as the author of the "G.I. Bill of Rights," was also an outstanding Stockton attorney, Commander of the Karl Ross Post of the American Legion, leader in the Opera Association, and supporter of many cultural and historical activities. The large main auditorium at Delta College was named for him after his death in 1976.

In 1950, Charles Hawkins set fire to a stack of Kleenex boxes to show how he felt about the "Fair Trade Laws." As a result he was in several court actions in the late 1940s. He won a court trial after an actual fist fight with Board of Equalization members for selling beer below the "Fair Trade" price. Hawkins was a member of the County Board of Supervisors, and owned and operated the "Bigg and Littel" store on the Waterloo road. He was killed in a shooting accident in the store in 1965.

Fred Feary won the bronze medal at the Olympics held in Los Angeles in August 1932. He had fought in amateur fights throughout the Valley and in San Francisco. In sixty-eight matches, he won sixty-four by knockouts and lost two.

Ralph Yardley, creator of the "Remember When" series that appeared daily for decades in the Stockton Record. Mr. Yardley was a photographer, too, and recorded many historical scenes with his camera. A large collection of Yardley drawings was given to the Pioneer Museum and Haggin Galleries, and selections are on public view.

Eddie Le Baron, great College of the Pacific football star of the 1940s, achieved national recognition.

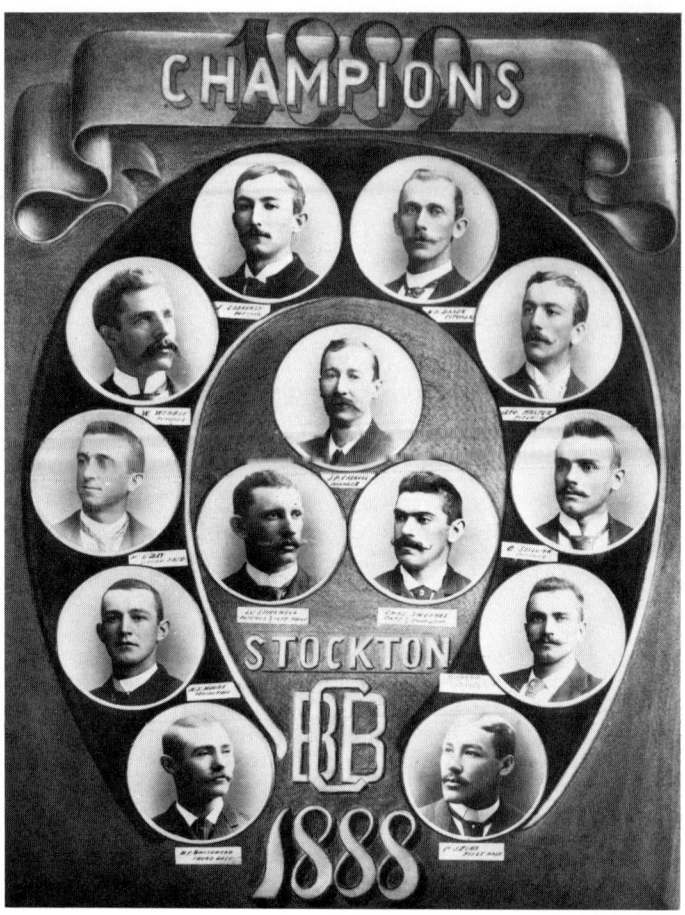

Stockton baseball champions of 1888. Notice that all but two have mustaches.

Cy and Bill Moreing's famous "Outlaws" baseball team of 1908. This picture was taken at Oak Park. The Outlaws won national recognition in a war with organized baseball, about the time the National and American Leagues were formed. There were many problems regarding rules, regulations, salaries, etc. The Outlaws were a superior ball club and won ninety-five percent of all the games they played, including some against professional teams from the East. Standing, from left to right: Hal Chase, super first baseman (played for New York, American League); Bill Moreing, centerfielder; Ben Henderson, pitcher; Danny Shay, infielder (played for New York and St. Louis). Seated: Bill Moriarty, shortstop; Joe Joyce, third baseman; Jim Smith, outfielder; Cy Moreing, manager; Charles Campbell, infielder; Tom Hackett, catcher; "Doc" Moskeman, pitcher; Ravi Gianelli, mascot.

(CHICAGO 2, STOCKTON 2)
AT STOCKTON, ON THURSDAY, NOV. 8, 1888

(BANNER ISLAND GROUNDS, SOUTHWEST FROM CORNER OF FREMONT & MONROE STREETS)

CHICAGO

	AB	R	H	O	A	E
Ryan, cf	4	0	1	3	0	0
Pettitt, rf	4	0	0	0	0	0
Sullivan, lf	4	1	1	2	0	1
Anson, 1b	4	1	2	13	1	1
Pfeffer, 2b	4	0	1	4	6	0
Williamson, ss	4	0	0	0	3	1
Burns, 3b	4	0	1	0	0	0
Tener, p	4	0	0	0	7	0
Daley, c	4	0	1	5	0	0
	36	2	7	27-	17-	3

STOCKTON

	AB	R	H	O	A	E
Moore, cf	4	1	0	1	0	0
Whitehead, 3b	4	1	1	2	4	0
Howard, rf	4	0	1	0	0	0
Sweeney, ss	4	0	1	4	5	1
Stockwell, c	3	0	0	3	1	0
Baker, lf	3	0	0	1	0	0
O'Day, 2b	3	0	0	0	3	0
Selna, 1b	3	0	0	16	0	0
Harper, p	3	0	0	0	4	0
	31	2	3	27	17	1

The Chicago club, under the captaincy of the famous slugger Cap Anson, had just finished in 2d place in the National League race, stopping over in San Francisco on their way to Australia for exhibitions. The "Father of Baseball," Al G. Spaulding, was touring with the Chicagos, and all were quartered at the famous Baldwin Hotel in San Francisco. In San Francisco they played on the old Haight St. grounds

Cap Anson was 1888 batting champion, National League, while pitcher Tener was later governor of Pennsylvania & president of National League

Pitcher Geo. Harper went up to the Brooklyn Nationals in the 1890's, and later umpired in the old California League for Stockton games, then operated a tailor shop in Stockton. Whitehead also went up to majors, while Stockton's other catcher, Geo. Stallings, eventually became the "Miracle Man" of the 1914 Boston Nationals, who came from last place in July to win the World Series. Stockton's Sweeney was the best short-stop in the California League, while Selna & O'Day were slick with glove

Above game called end of 9 innings on account of darkness & dust

FINAL STANDINGS, California League, 1888

	Won	Lost	Pct.
Stockton	40	25	615
Haverlys, S.F.	36	30	545
Pioneers, S.F.	31	37	455
Greenhood & Moran, Oakland	26	41	388

(By Walter Kientz, with help of 1888 S.F. 'Call' & Stockton 'Independent')

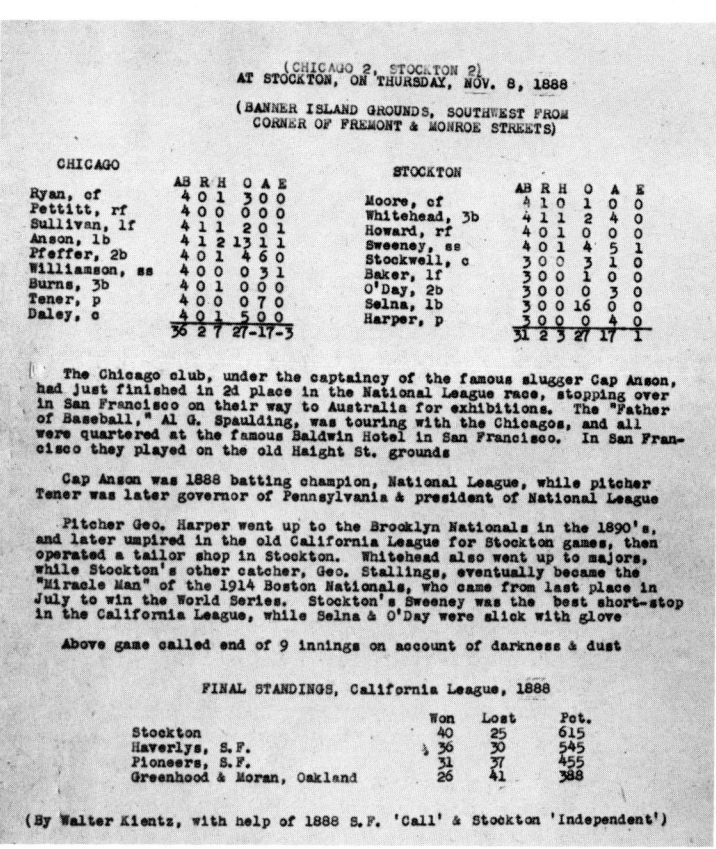

Scoreboard write-up in the baseball game of November 8, 1888 between Stockton and Chicago. Many world records in sports were broken in Stockton or by Stocktonians. Eric Knenz held the world's record for the discus toss in 1930. The race horse "Sunol" broke the world trotting record at the Stockton track on October 29, 1891. Stockton had a famous kite-shaped track where world trotting records were broken between 1890 and 1895. Other early-day sports stars were "Jules" Frankenheimer, star halfback for Stanford in 1895. Oscar Stange was catcher for the Detroit Tigers in Ty Cobb's day. Carroll Grunsky was an outstanding hurdler of 1917. George Parker was the fastest human of his time; he went to compete in Australia. There were many more outstanding athletes in later years.

Famous Stockton High School coaches at a 1961 reunion. From left to right are Jim Cave, Pete Lenz, Fred Soloman, and Wallace McKay.

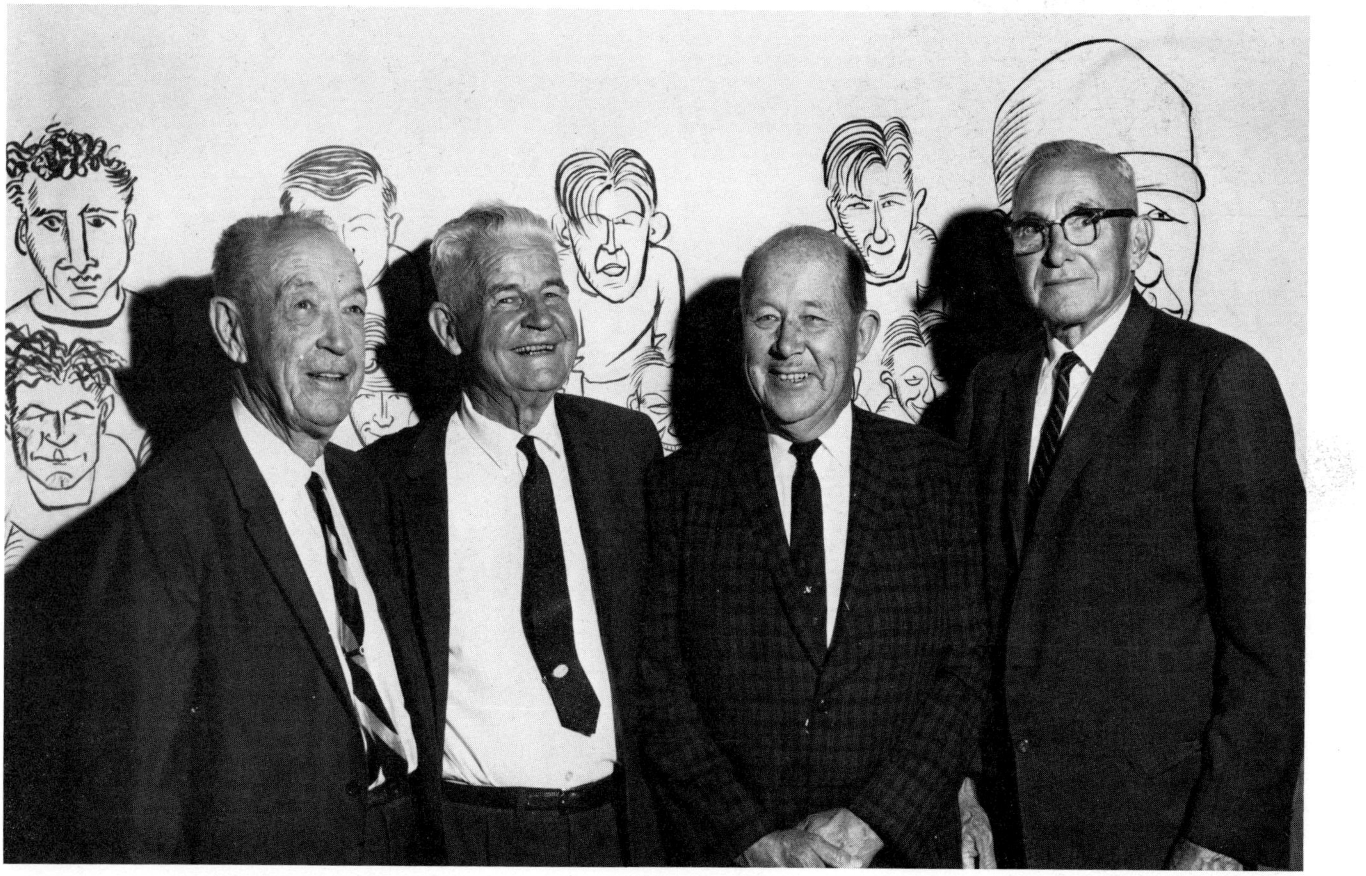

A routine geese and duck catch. In 1916 the limit was twenty-five birds per person, and for holders of a commercial license there was no limit. In this picture from left to right are Pete Piccolo, Ross Ghiorzio, and Victor Leonardini. Piccolo was operator of the New York Hotel and Restaurant, located on the northeast corner of Market and Aurora Streets (notice the menu on the side of the building.)

The famous race horse Sweepida at the county fairgrounds with Mrs. Harry C. Hill, left, whose husband owned the horse, and Mrs. Laurence Staples, wife of the trainer. The San Joaquin County Fair Association honored Sweepida by naming their feature race the Sweepida Handicap. Sweepida died May 8, 1970 at the age of thirty-three and is buried near the main entrance to the grandstand. A granite stone marks the spot. He is remembered as one of the nation's greatest race horses.

Sweepida, #8, winning the 1940 $50,000 Santa Anita Derby. In the top left Sweepida with jockey Ralph Neves in the winner's circle. To the right, Harry "Dutch" Hill, Stockton sportsman, gambler, and owner of Sweepida, receives the gold cup and $18,000 grand prize. Sweepida paid $68.60 to win, $21.00 to place, and $1.10 to show. He went on to win more than $100,000 in his lifetime.

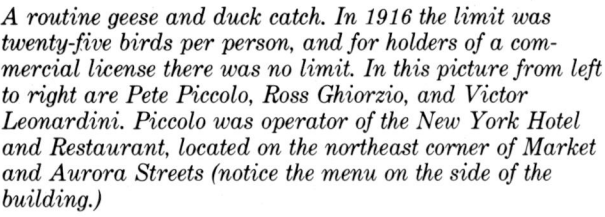

The picture shows the first Clements Stampede and Rodeo in 1946. Clements is east of Stockton on Highway 88. The show is now an annual event attended by hundreds of spectators and participants, including many Stocktonians.

A great American pastime during the Depression was "pee wee golf." Stockton had several courses. The one shown was in the parking area of the Hotel Clark on Sutter Street.

Index

Abbott, A. M., *89*
Acacia Street, *86,133,144*
Ackermann, Rabbi, *144*
Adams, Maude, *145,147,148*
Agricultural Hall, *54,60,137-38,140*
Agricultural Society, 53
Air Forces Advanced Training School, *38*
Airport Way, *65*
Alemany, Archibishop, 139
Alexander, R. L., 15
Alice (tug boat), *19*
All the King's Men, 151
Alpine Avenue, *9*
Althouse Eagal Company, *8*
Amador (boat), 26
Amador County, 104
American Legion, *123,165*; Karl Ross Post, *165*
American Legion Park, *38*
American River, 39
American Street, *4,43,50,51,119,150*
Amtrak, *37*
Anderson ranch, *94*
Anderson Street, 60
Ansbro, Martin, *72*
Apos, Tom, *51*
Appel, William E., *150*
"Arks," *23*
Arlington, the, *51*
Armbrust, Louis, *43*
Ashe, Dr. R. Porter, *59,71*
Ashley, Charles, 81
Asparagus, *87,88,89-90,92*
Atherton, Warren, *103,107,165*
Atlanta Falcons, *112*
Aurora Street, *44,60,153,168*; South, *161*
Austin Brothers Hardware, 4
Avenue Stable, *43*
Avon Theater, *145,149*

B Street, *161*
Bacon Island, *92,98*
Ballin' the Jack, *147*
Balloon ascension, *62,62*
Bank of America, *41,47,86*
Bank of Italy, *41,47*
Bank of Stockton, *41,47,105,141*
Banner Island, *158*
Barnett, Hal, *164*
Barth, Rodell K., 80
Bateman, Dr. E. B., *99,128*
Bates, Blanche, *145,148*
Baun, Ted, *102*
Baxley, Barbara, *113*
Baxter Stadium. See College of the Pacific
Beachy, Lincoln, *28,38*
Belding Building, *45*

Bell, Alexander Graham, 117
Bellota, California, *91*
Belt, Alcalde George Gordon, 59-60
Benicia, California, 61
Benjamin Holt Drive, *13,47*
Bennett, Mel, *120*
Berkeley, California, 90
Berry, Laura, *70*
Best Tractor Company, 89
Bicentennial (1976), 62
Big Country, 146
"Big Four," *27,35*
Bigg and Littel Store, *165*
Big Red Cars, *28,33*
Birney-type streetcars, *33*
Bishop, California, *111*
Bissell, J. M., 139
Black, Alexander, *46*
Black Bart, *74,75*
Black Grocery Stores, *46*
Black, Houston, *46*
Blaive, Father Dominic, 139
Blake, Moffitt & Towne warehouse, *19*
Blanchard, Dr. Joseph, 103-4,*108*
Blood Alley, 146
Blossom, Andrew, *49*
Board of Education, 99-100
Board of Equalization, *165*
Board of Supervisors. See San Joaquin County
Bob In, the, *52*
Bohemian Bar, *154*
Booth, Edwin, *145,149*
Bortalazzo, Dr. Julio, 104
Bours and Company, *47*
Bours, B., *47*
Bours, T. Robinson, Bank, *41,47*
Bradley, Dr. Burke, 103-4
Bragg Street, 60
Branch Slough, 17
Breuners, 3,*50*
Brewer, Kara Pratt, 101
Briare, Frank, *76*
Bridge Place, 80
Bridge Street, *48,73,77*
Brown DeMarcus, *113*
Brown, John, *70*
Brown, Pat, *67*
Brubeck, Dave, *147,152*
Bryan, William Jennings, 61,*66*
Budd, Governor James A., *61,61,65,66,*103
Budd House, *65*
Budd, Joseph, 65
Buffum brothers, 116
Buffum, George, 116
Buhach, *44,162*
Bull, Cliff, *67*
Bull Pen, the, *155*

Burbank, Luther, 89,*98*,146,*152*
Burbank potato, 89,146
Burgess, Phil, *120*
Burke Bradley Drive, 103
Burnett, Governor Peter, 59
Burns, Dr. Robert E., 101-2,*107,111,113*
Burns Tower. See University of the Pacific
Burros, J. S., *120*

Calaveras County, *75*,104
Calaveras River, *13,*17-18,*24,70,*111,*156*; bridge, *123*
California Building, *47*
California History Foundation. See College of the Pacific; University of the Pacific
Californian, 115
California Navigation and Improvement Company, 26,*44,162*
California Paper Company, *43*
California State Fair, 53-54
California Steam Navigation Company, 26
California Street, *4,7,33,42,43,44,*81,*89,99, 105,*116,*119,121,*126-27,*130,149,160,161*; North, *33,43,44,147,152,154*; South, *43,45, 154*
California Theatre, *148*
California Traction Company, *28,33*
California Transportation Company, *31*
"California Zephyr" (train), *37*
Campbell, Charles, *166*
Campbell, Lindsay, *120*
Campe's, *51*
Candee, J. G., 116
Canlis, Michael N., *72,73*
Cannon, Martin, 80
Captain Sutter (riverboat), 26
Captain Weber (steamboat), 26
Carroll, James, 80
Carroll, Mike, *76*
Carroll, S.J., 138
Cassidy, Benjamin, *7*
Castle Street, *52*
Castle, Tom, and his Family Orchestra, 147
Caterpillar track-type tractor, *41,*55,*64,*88-89,*95,96,97*
Caterpillar Tractor Company, 89
Catholic Church, 139. See also St. Mary's Church
Cave, Jim, *167*
Caviglia's Night Hawks, 147
Cecchetti, Julio, *77*
Cemetery Lane, *68*
Centennial (1876), *44,62,70,162*
Center Street, 1,*12,13,30,36,44,46,47,*54,60 *77,79-*80,*82,*99,*106,107,*115-16,*126,149*
Central Exchange, 60

Central Fire Station, 57,85
Central Methodist Church, 6,45,138,141,164
Central Pacific Railroad, 1,26-27,35,37,75, 117
Chamber of Commerce, 100,128,146
Channel Street, 3,42,44,45,55,56,60,65,72, 74,116-17,122,160; East, 83
Charleston the, 147
Charter Way, East, 94
Chase, Hal, 166
Chase, Steve, 120
Chastain, Harold, 112
Cherokee Lane, 33
Children's Home, 57
Childs, Cy, 75,77
Chinatown, 41,52,106
Chinese community, 52,73,106
Church Street, 57,82,161
Cinderella (dance hall), 147
Citizens Police, 71
City Council, 1,42,62,79-81,99
City Hall, 12,13,23,60,73,76,77,139,151
City Manager, 18,24,70
Civic Center, 12,13,54-55
Civic Memorial Auditorium, 12,13,30,54, 73,152,160
Civil War, 115
Claiborn, C. B., 47
Clam shell dredging bucket, 44,89
Clark, Dr. Asa, 127,132
Clark, Dr. Fred, 127
Clark Sanitarium, 132
Clements, California, 169
Clements, Charles, 96
Clements Stampede and Rodeo, 169
Clifton, James, 80
Club Lido, 147
Cobb, Ty, 167
Coconut Grove, 147
Cohn, A. B., 50
Colberg Boat Works, 68,69
College of the Pacific, 2,100-103,107,109, 110,111,112,113,152,166; Anderson Dining Hall, 111; Baxter Stadium, 102,112; Board of Regents, 100,102; California History Foundation, 110; Christian Education Unit, 109; Conservatory of Music, 109; Irving Martin Library, 102,110; Morris Chapel, 109; Pacific Memorial Stadium, 102; School of Expression, 113; School of Music, 109; Smith Memorial Gate, 109. See also University of the Pacific
Colt, Edwin, 80
Colton, Walter, 115
Columbia, California, 113
Columbia House Hotel, 45,48
Columbia State Park, 113
Columbia Theatre, 113
Combined harvester, 41,55,88,96
Commerce Street, 81,89
Commercial Bank, 86; building, 47,86
Commercial Hotel, 48
Commercial Record, 115
Coney Island Chili Parlor, 51
Coney Island Restaurants, 51
Cool Hand Luke, 146
Coolidge, President Calvin, 15
Coolures, Mitchell, 80
Copperopolis, California, 27
Copper ore, 27
Corinthian Building, 1,3,53,55,116
Corral Hollow, 44
Corwin, James, 137
Cotton Club, 147
Country Club Boulevard, 8,57
Courthouse. See San Joaquin County
Court of Sessions, 59-60
Coxey's Army, 158
Crabtree, Lotta, 145,149

Craig, John, 76
Crawford, Broderick, 151
Crocker, William H., 67
Crosstown Freeway, 10,13,54
Crudeli, Morris, 92
"Cunningham's Castle," 72,74,75
Cunningham, Thomas, 72-73,72,74,75,103, 158

Daisy Gray (ship), 16,20,123
Dallas Cowboys, 112
Dameron Hospital, 127-28,132,133
Dameron, Dr. J. D., 127-28,132
Damon, Rev. James C., 137
"Dan and Warfield," 148
Davis, John S., Company, 89
Deep Water Bonds, 15
Deep Water Channel, 62,69
Deep Water Project, 15,18,19
Delta King (riverboat), 26-27,31,44
Delta Queen (riverboat), 26,31,44
DeMille, Cecil B., 146
Denig, William "Pony," 115
Dennis, C. M., 109
Depression, the, 101,169
Detroit Tigers, 167
Devaney, George, 46
Dewey, J. J., 126
Dewey, Jim, 77
DeYoung, C. K. "Bird," 164
DeYoung Memorial Chapel, 164
DeYoung, Mike, 164
Diablo, Mount, 19
Diamond Sunsweet, 94
Diamond Walnut Growers, Inc., 94
Dick's Drive In, 52
District Fair Association, 140
Ditz, George, 107
Diverting Canal, 17
Dominican Sisters, 127
Dowell, Lillie, 96
Dowell, Ora, 96
Downtown, 1-3,7,14,81,160
Drake, Don, 120
Dreamland Ballroom, 123,147
"Drifted Snow Flour," 88
Duning, Arthur, 150
Dutschke, Westley, 76

E Street, 123
Earl, John, 120
East Side Presbyterian Church, 148
Eaten, R. S., 120
Eclipse (side-wheeler), 19
Eden Square Apartments, 86
Edison High School, 132
Edison Street, 60
Edsel, 34
Eiler, A. E., 120
El Dorado Brewing Company, 41,51
El Dorado School, 106,142
El Dorado Street, 1,6,10,12,13,19,29,30,33, 42,44,47,49,52,55,55,56,57,66,77,79-80,86, 106,116,128,135,138-39,142,143,145,149, 152,153,155,161; bridge, 19; North, 162; South, 48
Ellsworth, Myra, 120
El Placer Theater, 149
El Rancho del Campo de los Franceses, 17
Elsom, William, 43,120
Emmett Guard Band,70
Episcopal Church, 139,143. See also St. John's Church
Erb, Charles "Boots," 112
Esbach, K. V., 76
Escalon, California, 91
Esquire Theater, 148,150
Eugenia Street, 162
Euphemia (ship), 125
Eureka Company, 80-82; Engine #2, 83
Evans, Gil, 147

Fairgrounds. See San Joaquin County
Fair Trade Laws, 165
Fallon House Theatre, 113
Fallon, Jim, 113
Family Grocery Store, 46
Farmers and Merchants Bank, 47
Farnsworth, J., 120
Fat City, 146
Feary, Fred, 165
Federal Deposit Insurance Corporation, 120
Fee, Patrick, 43
Ferguson, June, 103
Fern Island, 20
Ferrell, F. E., 43
Ferrell, F. E., and Company, 40,43
Fetzer, Jacob, 49
Field, Stephen, 35
Filipino Center, 2
Finnell, Mike, 76
First Baptist Church, 142
First Congregational Church, 45,141
First National Bank, 140
Five Mile House, 17,52. See also Otto's
Flaco, Juan. See Brown, John
Floods, 17-18,30,122,157,160; 1890, 156; 1893, 159; 1907, 17,160; 1955, 18,160
Flora Street, 60,107; West, 100
Foley, W. H., 146
Folsom, California, 5
Folsom Prison, 75
Football Coaches Association, 101
Forty-Nine Drug Company, Inc., 135
Fox California Theater, 146,148
Fox West Coast, 148
Francis Goes to West Point, 150
Frankenheimer, Jules, 167
Franklin School, 99,106,107
Freedom Train, 62
Fremont, Jessie, 145
Fremont, John C., 145
Fremont Street, 30,54,144,153
French Camp, California, 72,74,75,93,127, 129
Fresno, 27
Friedberger, Dr. William, 127
Frosharg, Hank, 120
Fulton Street, 141

Galendo, Tony, 120
Galgiani, Oscar, 162
Galgiani, Vincent, 162
Gallagher, Father Joseph, 139
Geddings and Hartwell, 89
General Motors, 44
George Washington University, 112
Ghiorzio, Ross, 168
Gianelli, Ravi, 166
G. I. Bill of Rights, 165
Gill, Joseph, 76
Gillespie, Captain, 70
Giraffe Hotel, 60
God's Little Acre, 146
Golden Gate (ship), 20
Gold rush, 25,39-40,59,71,79,99,125,135, 137,140,145
Gold Rush Restaurant, 51
Goodman, Benny, and his Orchestra, 147
Goodwin, Rev. George, 141
Googie and his Dragons, 154
Gott, Gail (Scheere), 150
"Governor Stanford" (locomotive), 27,35
Governor's Mansion, 65
Graham, Mary, 129
Grain, 16-17,20,21,22,39-41,88-89,91
Grain Elevators, 16,20,21,22
Grand Central Hotel, 48,160,162
Grand Triumphal Arch, 70
Grant Street, 126
Grant, Ullysses S., 48
Grapes, 87,88,95,162

Gravtzow, Fred, 75
Grunsky, Carroll, 167
Grunsky, Lottie, 107
Guild Hall, 139,143
Guntert and Zimmerman, 161

Hackett, Tom, 166
Hagar, Rev. E., 139
Haggin Galleries. See Pioneer Museum and Haggin Galleries
Haines-Houser combined harvester. See combined harvester
Hale Department Store, 50
Hall, Clark, 120
Hall of Records, 121
Hammer Lane, 52,85
Hammond and Yardley Grocery Store, 45
Hammond, R. P., 55
"Happy Days," 146
Harding-Cox election, 118
Harding Way, 5,9,52,105,106,161; East, 52,107
Harkins, Al, 8
Harkins, Con, 43
Harkins, Con, Blacksmith Shop, 43
Harriman, Rev. Orlando, 139
Harris, Matteson and Williamson, 89
Harrison Street, 133; North, 31
Hart's Lunch, 41,51
Hart, William S., 151
Harty, Frank, 72
Hawkins, Charles, 165
Hazel Kirke, 149
Hazelton Avenue, 82,127,128
Hazelton Library, 55,57
Hazelton, Dr. William, 55,57
Headreach Island, 20
Held, Ann, 148
"Helvetia Gardens," 162
Hemet Avenue, 85
Henderson, Ben, 166
Henderson, M. P., 39
Henderson, M. P., and Son, 42
Henry Apartments, 57
Hickinbotham Brothers, 39,161
Hickinbotham, Donald E., 161
Hickinbotham, Edwin, 161
Hickinbotham, John, 161
Hickinbotham, Ralph W., 161
Highway 50, 160
Highway 88, 169
Highway 99, 10,13
Hill, Andrew R., 103
Hill, Harry "Dutch," 168
Hill, Mrs. Harry C., 168
Hillman, Frank, 161
Hillman, Raymond W., vii
Hillman-Rindge mansion, 161
Hoffman Saloon, 122
Hogan Dam, 18,24
Hogan Reservoir, 70
Hogan, Walter, 18,24,70
Holden Drug Company, 32,122,128,135
Holden, Erastus S. ("Doc"), 53,128,135
Holiday Inn, 3,19
Holt, Benjamin, 55,88,103
Holt Brothers. See Holt Manufacturing Company
Holt, Charles, 88
Holt Manufacturing Company, 41,88-89,95,96,97,152
Holt Memorial Hall, 55
Holt track-type tractor. See Caterpillar track-type tractor
Honeychurch, Lillian, 150
Hoover, President Herbert, 107
Hoover School, 107
Hotel Clark, 49,169
Hotel Philson, 86
Hotel Stockton, 6,41,49,61,73,153,159

Hotel Wolf, 49
Houser-Haines, 55,89
Howell Taxi Company, 27
Hughes Airwest, 28
Hughes, Charles Evans, 61,67
Hughes, Mrs. Charles Evans, 67
Hunt, Dr. Rockwell D., 110
Hunter Square, 1,11,17,53-54,60,62,62,63,66,136,147. See also the Plaza
Hunter Street, 5,47,55,56,57,60,74,80-82,90,115,119,127,139,142,144,155; North, 50; South, 83
Hyatt, C. G., 44

Imperial Hotel, 41,48
Influenza epidemic, 128,136
Inglis, William, 164
Insane Asylum of the State of California, 126
Interstate 5, 13
Invincible (boat), 26
Iowa, 87
Ireland, John, 151
Iron ore, 16,17,21

J. D. Peters (steamboat), 26,30,44,162
The Jack Knife Man, 146,151
Jackson, John, 76
Jackson Natural Gas Well Baths, 146,153
Jack Tone Road, 17,163
Jail. See San Joaquin County
James, Harry, band, 147
Japan, 17,21,98
Japan Air Line, 38
Jarvis Shipyards, 30
Jefferson Street, 44
Jenny Lind (side-wheeler), 26
Jewish Synagogue, 144
Johnnie's Waffle Shop, 41,52
Johnson, Congressman Leroy, 67
Johnson, President Lyndon, 120
Jones and Hewlett, 90
Jones, J. Frank, 150
Jones tract, 94
Joyce, Joe, 77,166
Julia (boat), 26
Junior Auxiliary, 131

Kahn, Dr. Sy, 113
Karras, Tom, 51
KDKA, 118
Keane, Dr. James, 104
Kech, Al, 154
Keeling, Francis F., 67
Kelsey, Dr. J. M., 47
Kennedy, Mrs. Gerald, 156
Kensington Way, 103
Kerr, Captain George, 115
Kerr, John C., Ranch, 91
KGDM, 118
Kiechler, Bill, 164
King, Bill, 112
King of Kings, 146
King, Rev. Thomas Starr, 137
Kizer, Avery, 120
KJAX, 118
Kjeldsen, Chris, 112
KJOY, 6,118
Klench, Dan 76
Knenz, Eric, 167
Knights of Columbus, 164
Knoles, Dr. Tully C., 100-101,103,107,110,111,112
Knowles, Will H., 80
Korean War, 69
Kuchel, Senator Thomas, 67
Ku Klux Klan, 159
KUOP, 118
KWG, 118,123
Kyle and Company, 68,69

Lafayette School, 99
Lafayette Street, 10,56,57,82,107
Lakas, Gus, 51
Lamburth Ranch, 96
Lathrop, California, 1-2,27,35
Latimer, Rev. Donald R., 142
Latta, Dr. Samuel E., 127,128
Le Baron, Eddie, 102,112,166
Leigh, Janet, 146
Lenz, Pete, 167
Leonardini, Victor, 168
Le Tourneau, Robert, 89,163
Le Tourneau scraper, 89
Levee Street, 1,47,81,89
Levee, the, 116
Levinsky, Arthur, 67
Levinson's Bridal Shop, 47
Lewis, Tillie, 50,103
Lewis, Tillie, Foods, Inc., 40,50
Lincoln Grammar School, 105
Lincoln Highway, 106
Lincoln Hotel, 48
Lincoln Road, 108
Lincoln School, 105,108
Lincoln Street, 128,132,133
Lincoln Theater, 150
Lincoln Village, 2-3,13
Lincoln Village West, 13
Linden, California, 44,62,94
Lindsay Street, 57,99,116,144
Liquid Sugar Corporation, 19
"Little House on the Prairie," 146
Locke, Dr. Dean Jewett, 103,125
Lockeford, California, 91,125,163
Lodi, California, 28,33,95
Lodi High School, 33
Long, Thomas, 103
Los Angeles, 25,70,80,94,165; Revolt, 70
Lost Paradise, 147
Lottie Gronsky School, 107
Louis Park, 14,151; Dad's Point, 151
Lower Sacramento Road, 2,9,105,123,126
Lyman, Abe, band, 147
Lyons, George, 88
Lyric Theater, 150

MacDonald Island, 68
Macy's, 3
Maddens Delmonico's, 51
Madison School, 146
Madison Street, 9,84,88,150
Madjeska, 148
Magnolia Street, 128,132,133
Maguire's California Minstrels, 145
Mail Fountain, 47
Main Street, 1,4,5,6,7,14,29,32,36,41,46,47,50,53,60,66,79-81,83,85,86,89,90,99,116,128,135,138,140,142,145,148,149,150,152,161,163; East, 42,48,51,117,122,148,150
Malibu Beach, 147,153
Mallory, Harry, 120
Manchester, California, 120,147
Mandarin Theater, 150
Mandeville Island, 30
"Man Hunters," 146
Mansion House, 11
Manteca, California, 120,147
Marengo's, 147
Maria (ship), 20,25
Mariposa, California, 145
Mariposa Road, 94
Market Street, 35,49,52,54-55,57,74,77,80,99,116,119,121,126,142,155,168; East, 49,161
Marshall, James, 39
Marshall, Oscar, 76
Martin, Irving, Jr., 119
Martin, Irving, Sr., 102,115-16,119
Martin, Mrs. Irving, Sr., 116
Martin, Irving III (Gully), 116,119
Martin, V. Covert, vii,8,163

Mary Garratt (steamboat), 26
Marysville, California, 53,117
Masonic Hall, 60,*162*
Masonic Temple, 6,54,*56,57*,118
Masons, 54,*63*
Massei, Ernie, *154*
Mathews, Dave, *33*
Mathews Road, *74*
Mathews, Scott, *120*
Matteoni's, 147,*154*
Mattie's, 147
McCaffrey, Dr. Stanley E., 102-3,*111*
McCann, Michael, 80,*86*
McClatchy Broadcasting, *123*
McCormack Bros. Wholesale and Retail Meat Market, *46*
McCrone, Dr. Alistair, 102
McDermott, Mat, *76*
McFall, Congressman John, *120*
McGaven, Darren, *113*
McGlothen, *75*
McGough, Father W. E., 140
McGurk, Charles, *76*
McHugh, Frank, *77*
McKay, Wallace, *167*
McKinley Park, 146,*153*
McKinley, President William, 61,*67*
McKinley, Mrs. William, *67*
McLeod Lake, 1,*3*,12,*13,23,30*
McNish Building, 60,72
Medico-Dental Building, *123*
Merced County, 44
Merchants, Manufacturers and Employers Association, 158
Merrill, Inez A., *61*
Methodist Church, 137-38,*140*. See also Central Methodist Church
"Mexico City Joe's" Restaurant, *108*
Michelotti, Carl, *135*
Micke Grove, *95*
Milky Way (malt shop), *8*
Miller, William P., 39,*42*
Mills College, 100
Milo, *20*
Milton, California, 27,*36*
Mineral Baths, *153*
Miner Avenue, 17,*47*,138-39,*140,141,143*
Miner Slough, 17
Miracle Drive In, *52*
"Miracle Mile," 2,*9*
The Miracle Worker, 150
Mississippi River, 27
"Miss Polly," *108*
Model T Ford, *6*
Mokelumne River, 90
Monday Nighters, 152
Monroe Street, 150
Monterey, 59,115
Monteverdi, Roland, *154*
Montgomery Ward, 3
Moore Equipment, *69*
Moreing, Bill, *166*
Moreing, Cy, *166*
Moriarty, Bill, *166*
Mormon Channel, *16,43*
Mormon community, 40
Mormon Slough, 17,*25,160*
Morris Chapel. See College of the Pacific
Morris, Harry, *75*
Morris, Mr. and Mrs. Percy F., *109*
Moskeman, "Doc," *166*
Mother Lode, 27,*39*-40,*48,72,113,125*,147
"Mountain Freighter," *29*
Mt. Vernon House, *142*
Mr. D's Pizzaria, *42*
Mr. Roberts, 150
Multi-Lingual Multi-Cultural Center, *107*
Municipal Baths, *153*
Murphy, Helen, *156*
Murphy, M. D., 80,*86*

Murphys Cornet Band, 147
Musicians Union Local 189, 147

Nagel, Mr. and Mrs. John, *34*
Napa State Hospital, 126
National Register of Historic Places, 100, *106*
National Sheriffs Association, 73
National Theater, *150*
Naval Annex, 62
Navy V-12 program, 101
Neagle, David, *35*
Nevada, 17,*21*
Nevada City, California, *111*
Neves, Ralph, *168*
Newby's Drive Inn, *52*
Newman, John, *120*
New York Hotel and Restaurant, *3,168*
New York Yankees, *118,166*
Nielson, Clyde, *150*
Nixon, Richard, 62,*67*
North Stockton, 5,*13,33,50,122,123*,126
North Street, *9*
Nuttman, James, 79-80

Oakdale, *36*,102,*112*
Oakland, 27,*70*
Oak Park, 5,*97,166*
Oak Street, *42,51,55,57*
Oard, Paul, 118
Oard Radio Laboratories, 118
O'Connor, Father W. B., 127,*130*
Odd Fellows Lodge, 54,*63*
Ohio River, 27
O'Keefe, Jack, 73,*77*
Oklahoma Crude, 146
Oldfield, Barney, 27
Old Hogan Dam, 18,*24*
Olympic Baths, *153*
Olympics, *165*
On Lock Sam's, 41,*52*
Opera Association, *165*
Ophir Street, *65*
Oregon City, 25
Orsi's, M., Grocery, *45*
Orton, Dwayne, 103
Ospital Ranch, *91*
Ospital Road, *91*
Otto, Mr., *52*
Otto's, 17,*52*. See also Five Mile House
Oullahan, Mayor Alex, 89,146,*152*
Our Miss Brooks, 146
Our Town, 146
Outdoor Theatre, *113*
Outlaws, *166*
Owen, Cy, *107*
Owen, Rev. Isaac, *140*
Owl Drug Store, *7*

Pacific Avenue, 2,*8,9,13,47,52*,104,*105,106*, *108,123,138,141*
Pacific Fleet, *162*
Pacific Hospital, *132*
Pacific Little Theatre, *113*
Pacific Memorial Stadium. See College of the Pacific
Pacific Reserve Fleet, *69*
Pacific Southwest Airlines, 28
Pacific Tannery, *42*
Pacific Telephone and Telegraph Company, 118,*122*
Packwood, Nellie, *96*
Palm Street, *52*
Pappas, Tom, *51*
Park Street, *51*
Parker, George, *167*
Parker's Alley, 115,*119*
Parrot, the, *52*
Patton and Springer, 147
Pavilion, *10*,54,*56,61,67,82,84*,127

"Pee wee golf," *169*
Pelican Club, 147
Penney, J. C., 3,*4*
Peoria, Illinois, 89
Peters, California, *36,44*
Peters, J. D., 40,*44,70,162*
Peyton, Valentine Mason, 99
Piccolo, Pete, *168*
Piggly Wiggly, *8*
Pilgrim Street, *57,83,84*; North, *57*
Pioneer Museum and Haggin Galleries, vii, 55,*61,81,163,165*
Pioneer or Perish, 101
Pittsburgh, Pennsylvania, 118
Pixie Woods, *14*
Play Box, the, *113*
Plaza, the, 1-2,*11,17,32,50,60,62,63,66*,80, 147. See also Hunter Square
Plecarpo, Joe, 2
Plymouth Rock, 147
Poc, George, *120*
Pollock Shipyards, *69*
Portable Wireless Telephone Company, 118
Portland, Oregon, 17,*22,62*
Portuguese Hall, 147
Post Office, *56*,115-16,*121*
Potato Day, 89,146,*152*
Potatoes, 89-90,*98*,146
Potter, Wilbur, *75,77*
Powell, Dr. Dewey, *164*
Powers, Tom, *43*
Presbyterian Church, *106*,137-38,*142*. See also East Side Presbyterian Church
President Lincoln (ship), 22
Prinze, Joe, *161*
Progress (boat), 26
Promontory Summit, Utah, 27
Pump Room, *155*
Purdy, Samuel, 60

Quyle, Paul, *75*

Randall, A. H., 99
Red Cross, *136,160*
Reid, Dr. Robert K., 125-26
Relief Windmill Manufacturers, 89
Remington, Ben, *120*
Reynolds, Delbert, *75*
Reynolds, Rev. John, 139
Rialto Theater, *150*
Ribarsky, Randy, *152*
Richetti, Vincent "Googie," *154*
Riecks, William H., *72*
Righter, Erwin "Swede," *112*
Rindge, Fred, *161*
Rindge tract, *68*
Rio Vista, California, 27
Ripon, California, 40,*163*
Ritz Theater, *150*
Rizo, Spiro, *51*
Roberts Island Farm Bureau Hall, 147
Robinhood Drive, *123*
Rogers, Bill, *120*
Rogers, Will, 146,*148,151*
Rolt, Israel, 80
Roosevelt, President Franklin D., *121,165*
Roosevelt Street, East, *163*
Rose Street, *52*
Rotary convention, 30
Rothenbush family, *48,51*
Roth Road, 17
Rough and Ready Island, 62,*69*
Royal Shaving Parlor, 50
Rural Cemetery, *68*
Russ House, *48,162*
Russell, Lillian, 148
Ruth, Babe, 118
Rutherford, Newton, *76*

Sacramento, 26-28,*31,35*,53,*61,81*,101,*112*,

117,125,*158*; Port of, 17
Sacramento County, 104
Sacramento General Hospital, 126
Sacramento River, 27,*31*
Sacramento Street, *33,35,36*
Sacramento Valley, 87
Sagamore (steamer), *19*
St. Charles Hotel, 41,*48*
St. John's Church, 139,*143*
St. Joseph's Home, 127
St. Joseph's Hospital, 127-28,*130,131*; School of Nursing, 127,*130*
St. Mary's Church, *10*,54,139-40,*143*
Salt Lake City, 27
Salvation Army, *160*
Samson Iron Works, 41,*44*
Samson Tractor, *44*
San Andreas Independent, 115
San Francisco, 2,25-27,*30,31*,40-41,53,*67*, 71,79-81,90,116-17,125-26,138,*158,165*; airport, *38*; earthquake,*52*; Fire Department, 81
San Francisco and San Joaquin Valley Railroad, 27
San Francisco Bay, 62,*68,70*
San Francisco Vigilance Committee, 71
San Joaquin (boat), 26
San Joaquin County, 28,*38*,40,59-61,*63*, 71,*72*,75,87,88,90,*91*,93,*94*,*95*,103-4,*159*; Administration Building, 2,*64*; Assessor, *50*; Board of Supervisors, 59,61,*64*,72,*165*; Bureau of Criminal Identification and Investigation, *72*; courthouse, 1,2,*49*,53,60-61,*63,64*,76,*159,163*; Courts and Administration Building, *64*; Fair Association, *168*; Fairgrounds, *38*,146,*168*; hospital. See San Joaquin General Hospital; jail, 6, *45*,60,*72,74,75*; Welfare Department, *49*
San Joaquin Delta, 15,*20*,25,40,*44*,*68*,87-90, *92*,*98*,146
San Joaquin Delta College, vii,*13*,50,*72*,90, *98*,102-4,*108,111*,126,*165*; Atherton Auditorium, 103,*165*; Blanchard Gymnasium, 103; Board of Trustees, 104; Budd Center, 103; Cunningham Center, 103; Ferguson Pool, 103; Holt Center, 103; Lewis Little Theater, 103; Locke Center, 103; Shima Center, 103
San Joaquin Engine Company #3, *79*,81,*83*
San Joaquin General Hospital, 127-28,*128*, *129,132*
San Joaquin Hotel, *108*
San Joaquin Lodge #19 F. & A.M., *164*
San Joaquin Republican, 115
San Joaquin River, 1,*14*,17,25-26,*31*,39,79, 89
San Joaquin Street, 6,*14*,*36*,*45*,47,50,53,*56*, 60,*72,74*,80,82,*85*,*89*,*99*,*105*,116-17,*121*, *122*,137-38,*140*,*141*,*142*,145,*148*,*163*; North, 118,*122*; South, *37,48,152,153*
San Joaquin Valley, 87
San Joaquin Valley Agricultural Association, *10*,53-54,*56,135*
San Joaquin Valley Bank, 41,*47*
San Jose, 100,137,146,*156*
San Jose State University, 100
San Leandro, California, 89
San Pedro, California, 25
Santa Ana Derby, *168*
Santa Clara (steamer), 26
Santa Fe Hospital, 82
Santa Fe Railroad, 27,*37,48*
Sawyer, Gertie, *96*
Saxton, Rev. J. B., *142*
Schumann-Heink, Madame Ernestine, 118, *123*
Sears Roebuck and Company, 3
Sells Floto Company, 146
Selma, Alabama, *158*
Semmering, Larry, 102,*112*

Semple, Robert, 115
Sharpe Army Depot, 17
Shaw, H. C., Plow Company, 89
Shay, Danny, *166*
Shepherd and Green, Contractors, *86*
Shima, George, 89-90,*98*,103; Ranch, 89,*98*
Shippee, 89
Shippee, L. U., 54
Shrine Circus, *152*
Shurtleff, Dr. George A., 126
Sibley, Walter F., *72*
Sierra Nevada Mountains, 39
Sierra Theater, *150*
Silva, Manlio, *149*
Simpson, William, *76*
Sink, Rev. Reuben H., *141*
"Skid Row," 2,*10*,*48*,55
"Slow, Tired and Easy" Railroad. See Stockton Terminal and Eastern Railroad
Smith and Lang, *50,85*,138
Smith, C. O., *75*,*77*
Smith Canal, 8
Smith, Elmer, *75*
Smith, Frank Thornton, *49,152*
Smith, Grover, *77*
Smith, J. C., Company, 100
Smith, Jim, *166*
Smithsonian Institution, 55
Smythe, Dr. Margaret, 127,*128*
"Soda-Water Wagon," 81
Solano County, 104
Soloman, Fred, *167*
Sonora, California, *29,113*
Sonora Street, *161*; West, *85*
Sousa, Carlos A., *72,73*
Sousa, John Philip, *148*
Southern Mines, 1,25,*27*,*29*,39,79,125,137
Southern Pacific Railroad, 27,*33,35,36,37*, 61,*67,95*
Spanish American War Veterans, *68*
Speidel Company, 116
Speras, Kris, *51*
Sperry, Austin, 88
Sperry Flour Mill, *19*,40,*84*,88,*136*
Sperry, Nick, *51*
Spire, *5*
Spooner, John Pitcher, *6,163*
Spooner Studio, *163*
Sprague, Irving, *120*
Sprague, Tom, *120*
Stadium Drive, 103
Stagg, Amos Alonzo, 101-2,*110,112*
Stagg, Stella, 101
Stagnaro, Dave, *46*
Stagnaro, Frank, *46*
Stanford, Leland, 1,27
Stanford University, 100,*167*
Stange, Oscar, *167*
Stanislaus Street, *13*
Staples, Mrs. Laurence, *168*
Starweather, Professor, *62*
State Department of Food and Agriculture, 87
State of California Building, *55*
State Railroad Museum, *35*
State Theater, *148,149*,150
Steamboat 'Round the Bend, 146,*151*
Stephens Brothers Shipyards, *69*
Stephens Marine, *68*
Stevens, Elmer, *111*
Stevenson, Lyle, 80
Stewart, C. E., *40*
Stewart, D. R., *40*
Stewart, E. C., *40*
Stewart, Frank, *57*
Stockton Alameda and San Joaquin Railroad Company, *44*
Stockton Album Through the Years, vii,*163*
Stockton and Copperopolis Railroad, 2,27,*36*
Stockton Armory, *34*

Stockton Channel, 1-2,15,17,*19*,*20*,*22*,25,27, *30,31,36*,41,*44*,*48*,*49*,53-54,*56,57*,*62*,*68,69*, 147,*153,159*
Stockton City Lines, 28
Stockton Civic Theater, 146,*150*
Stockton College, 103,104. *See also* Stockton Junior College
Stockton Combined Harvester and Agricultural Works, 28
Stockton Cultural Heritage Board, *42,49*, *62,106*
Stockton Daily Argus, 115
Stockton Dry Goods Company, *50*
Stockton Electric Railroad, 28
Stockton Evening Mail, 47,116,*117*
Stockton Field, *38*,*67*
Stockton Fire Department, 81,82
Stockton gang plow, 41
Stockton Gas, Light and Heat Company, 82
Stockton Golf and Country Club, *8*,*57*
Stockton High School, *33,99*,*105,161,167*
Stockton Historical Landmark, *75,100*
Stockton House, 1,41,146
Stockton Independent, 115,*117*
Stockton Iron Works, *31*,40,*44*,89
Stockton Junior College, 103. *See also* Stockton College
Stockton Junior High School, *105*
Stockton Metropolitan Airport, 28,*38*,160
Stockton Naval Supply Depot, 69
Stockton Police Department, 73,*75*,*76,77*; Youth Activities, *37,73,77*
Stockton, Port of, 16-17,*20,21,22*,87,*123*; Ore docks, *21*; Port Director, 17,*22*
Stockton Record, *9*,100,102,115-16,*118,119*, *120*,*159,165*; "As the Sun Sets," *119*; Building, *123*; "Remember When," *165*
Stockton, Commodore Robert Field, 60,*70*, *162*
Stockton Rotary Club, *164*
Stockton Savings and Loan Bank, *47*
Stockton Savings and Loan Society, 41,*47*, *122*
Stockton Ship Canal Company, 15
Stockton State Hospital, 104,125-27,*128,132*
Stockton Steel Fabricators, *69*
Stockton Symphony Orchestra, *105*,147,*149*
Stockton Telephone Company, 117,*122*
Stockton Terminal and Eastern Railroad, *37*; Engine #1, *37*
Stockton Theater, 145,*149*
Stockton Unified School Board, 103
Stockton Unified School District, 103-4,*105*, *107*
Stockton Weekly Times, 115
Stockton Wheel Company, 88
Stone, Captain, *75*
Stone Pine tree, *162*
Stoultz, Vernon "Pop," *112*
Stoy, Herb, *120*
Stoyt, Arthur, *91*
Strand Theater, *150*
Stuart, Ernest, *75*
Studio Theatre, *113*
Sugar beets, 87,*89,94*
Suisun Bay, *22*
Sunol, *167*
Sunset Macaroni Factory, *46*
Sunset magazine, *109*
Sunset Telephone and Telegraph Company, 117,*122*
Superintendent of Schools, 99,103
Susanne (brig), 26,*72*,125
Sutter Street, *14*,*47*,*49*,*52*,54,*57*,*86*,*117*,*141*, *142*,*161*,*169*; North, 65,*155*; South, *51*,*52*
Swamp Act, 87
Sweepida, *168*
Sweepida Handicap, *168*

T and D Theater, *148*

T. C. Walker (steamboat), 26,*31*
Tadernarakis, Nick, *51*
Temple Israel Annex, *150*
Temple Israel Cemetery, *144*
Terry, David S., *35*
Tesla Coal Mines, *44*
Thacker, John, *75*
Thompson, Ralph E., 80,*86*
Thorn, Ben, *75*
Thrift, Eli, *120*
Tillie Lewis Theatre, *50*
Tinkham, George, 26
"Tin Lizzie," *34*
Tinsley Island, *20*
"Tin Villa," *161*
Tokay grapes, *95*
Tomatoes, 87,*88,93*
Tone, John H. "Jack," *163*
Tonseth, Ralph, *38*
Tracy, California, *44*
Transeastern (ship), *20*
Tretheway Block, *36*
Treuman, Lloyd, *112*
Tucker automobile, *34*
Tucker, Sophie, *148*
Tule Island, *20*
Tule Street, 60
Tuolumne County, *62*
Turkey Trot, 147
"Tuxedo Junction" (song), *8*
Tuxedo Park, 2,*8*
20-30 Club, *48*
Twiggs Street, 60
Tye, Hugh ("Judge Tye"), *77,120*

Under the Gaslight, *113*
Union Pacific Railroad, 27
Union Safe Deposit Bank, *40,99*
Union Street, *70,144*; North, 118
United Airlines, 28
U.S. Army Air Force, *38*
United States Hotel, *48*
University of California, 65,100,*112*
University of Chicago, 101,*110,112*
University of the Pacific, *13,57*,102-3,*109*, *111*,118,*128*,138,147; DeMarcus Brown Theatre, 102; Burns Tower, *13*,102,*111*; California History Foundation, *128*; Callison College, 102; Elbert Covell College, 102; Grace Covell Dormitory, *110*; Holt-Atherton Pacific Center for Western Studies, 103; Knoles Hall, *57*; Long Theatre, 103; Wendell Phillips Center, 102, *110*; Raymond College, 102; School of Education, 103; School of Pharmacy, 102; South Campus, *111*; Speech Arts Auditorium, 103; Stuart Library of Western Americana, 103,*163*; University College, 102; University Without Walls, 102; Donald Wood addition to the Irving Martin Library, 102. *See also* College of the Pacific
University of Santa Clara, 100
University of Southern California, 100,*110*
Utah, 17,*21*,27

Valley Brew Beer, 41,*51*
Valley Springs, California, 18,*70*
Van Fleet, Jo, *113*
Victoria Island, *92*
Victory Park, 55,81
Vidor, King, *151*
Vine Street, 99,*105,106*,138,*142*

Wagner, J. K., *46*
Wagner Meat Company, *46*
Walker, Walter, *76*
Wallace, B. C., Jr., *164*
Wallace, B. C., Mortuary, *164*
Wallace, Ben, *164*
Walla Walla, Washington, *96*
Walnut Association, *94*
Walnuts, *94*
Walnut Street, 127,*130*
Walsh, Thomas J., 82
Warren, Captain, 26
Washburn, Erv, 77
Washington Grammar School, *105*
Washington Park, *10*,54
Washington Redskins, *112*
Washington School, 99,*105*
Washington Square, 54
Washington Street, 35,*44*,56,82,99,*106,107*, 127,*139*; East, *143*; West, 15
Waterloo, California, *165*
Water wagons, *4*
Watson, Polly, band, 147
Webb's at the Stockton, *49*
Weber Avenue, 1,*6*,27,*33,36,43,45,47,*54,60, *70,79*-81,*88,89,97,108,116,123,136,137*, *140,145,148,149,153,158*; East, *33,45,46, 49,79*; West, *19,47,62,81,84,159*
Weber Bucket Brigade, 79
Weber, Captain Charles M., 1,*11*,17,25-26, 39,*53,55*,60,*62*,*62*,*79*-80,*99*-100,*126*,138-39,*144,156,157,162*; home, *19,139,143,156*; ship. *See Maria*; store, 1
Weber, Charles M., Jr., *156*
Weber, Charles M. III, *156*
Weber Engine Company #1, 79-81,*83*
Weber Fire House, *3,44*
Weber Gas Well Baths, *153*
Weber Hotel, *48*
Weber House, 116
Weber, Julia, *156*
Weber Point, 1,*19,62,142,156*
Weber Primary School, 100,*107*
Weberstown, 3,*13,156*
Weber, Thomas, *156*
Weinstock Hale, *50*
Weinstock Lubin, *50*
Weinstock's, 3,*50,85*
Wells Fargo and Company, *47,75*
West End Redevelopment, *10,73*
Western Pacific Railroad, 27,*37,85*
West Lane, 17,*52*,116,*156*
Wheeler, Lois, *113*
White, Edith Dunne, *149*
Whiteman, Paul, band, 147
Whitney, Jerry, *120*
Whittington, Bob, *120*
Wicker, Bob, 112
Wilhoit, Eugene, 100
Williams, Benjamin, 59-60
Willoughby, William H., 71
Willow Street, *150*
Wilson Way, *52,127,128,152,163*; South, *52*
Wilson, President Woodrow, 61,*67*
Windmills, *89*
Women's Auxiliary, *131*
Won, Dr. Kyung-Soo, *149*
Wood, Clyde, shipyard, *69*
Wood, Ethelyn, *70*
Wood, R. Coke, vii,*111*
Woods, Rev. James, 138,*142*
Woods, Mrs. James, 138
Woodward Island, *89,98*
World War I, 54,88-89
World War II, *38*,60,*62*,68,101,103,145,*161*
WPA program, *121*

Yardley, Ralph, *9,165*
Y.M.C.A., *111*
Yokuts Avenue, 104,*122*
Yolland, Charles W., *43*
Yolland Materials Company, *43*
Yosemite Building, *6,162,163*
Yosemite Cash Grocery Store, *45*
Yosemite Hotel, *162*
Yosemite House, 41,*48*
Yosemite Lake, *8*,146,*153*
Yosemite-Orpheum, *148*
Yosemite Street, North, *135*
Yosemite Theater, 145,*147,148,150*

Zallo Family, 147
Zeigler, Frank, *164*
Ziegler's Billiard Parlor, *117*
Zion Lutheran Church, *150*
Zuzallo's, *51*